ISBN 978-1-334-50997-1
PIBN 10630134

1 MONTH OF
FREE
READING

at

www.ForgottenBooks.com

By purchasing this book you are
eligible for one month membership to
ForgottenBooks.com, giving you
unlimited access to our entire
collection of over 700,000 titles via
our web site and mobile apps.

To claim your free month visit:

www.forgottenbooks.com/free630134

English
Français
Deutsche
Italiano
Español
Português

www.forgottenbooks.com

Mythology Photography **Fiction**
Fishing Christianity **Art** Cooking
Essays Buddhism Freemasonry
Medicine **Biology** Music **Ancient
Egypt** Evolution Carpentry Physics
Dance Geology **Mathematics** Fitness
Shakespeare **Folklore** Yoga Marketing
Confidence Immortality Biographies
Poetry **Psychology** Witchcraft
Electronics Chemistry History **Law**
Accounting **Philosophy** Anthropology
Alchemy Drama Quantum Mechanics
Atheism Sexual Health **Ancient History**
Entrepreneurship Languages Sport
Paleontology Needlework Islam
Metaphysics Investment Archaeology
Parenting Statistics Criminology
Motivational

IVAN PANIN.

Lectures

ON

RUSSIAN LITERATURE

PUSHKIN, GOGOL, TURGENEF,
TOLSTOY.

NEW YORK & LONDON:

G. P. PUTNAM'S SONS,

The Knickerbocker Press.

1889.

Copyright, 1889,

By Ivan Panin.

TO

MIRIAM

PREFACE.

—◆—

THE translations given in this volume, with the exception of the storm-scene from Tolstoy in the First Lecture, are my own.

The reader will please bear in mind that these Lectures, printed here exactly as delivered, were written with a view to addressing the ear as well as the eye, otherwise the book would have been entirely different from what it now is.

When delivering the Sixth Lecture, I read extracts from Tolstoy's " My Religion " and "What to Do," illustrating

every position of his I there commend ;
but for reasons it is needless to state,
I omit them in the book. I can only
hope that the reader will all the more
readily go to the books themselves.

I. P.

GRAFTON, MASS.,
     1 July, 1889.

CONTENTS.

———◆———

CONTENTS

LECTURE I.

INTRODUCTORY.

1. I HAVE chosen the four writers mentioned on the programme not so much because they are the four greatest names of Russian literature as because they best represent the point of view from which these lectures are to be delivered. For what Nature is to God, that is Literature unto the Soul. God ever strives to reveal himself in Nature through its manifold changes and developing forms. And the human soul ever strives to reveal itself in literature through its manifold changes and developing forms. But while to see the goal of the never resting creativeness of God is not yet given unto man, it is given unto mortal eyes to behold the promised land from Pisgah, toward which the soul

ever strives, and which, let us hope, it ever is approaching. For the soul ever strives onward and upward, and whether the struggle be called progress of species, looking for the ideal, or union with God, the thing is the same. It is of this journey of the soul heavenward that literature is the record, and the various chases of literary development in every nation are only so many mile-posts on the road.

2. In its childhood the human soul only exists; it can hardly yet be said to live; but soon it becomes conscious of its existence, and the first cry it utters is that of joy. Youth is ever cheerful, and in its cheer it sings. Youth sings to the stars in the sky, to the pale moon and to the red moon, to the maiden's cheeks and to the maiden's fan; youth sings to the flower, to the bee, to the bird, and even to the mouse. And what is true of the individual is equally true of the race. The earliest voices in the literature of any nation are those of song. In Greece Homer, like his favorite cicada, chirps right gladly, and in England Chaucer

and Shakespeare are first of all bards. In France and Germany it is even difficult to find the separate prominent singers, for there the whole nation, whatever hath articulate voice in it, takes to singing with its troubadours and minnesingers. In its earliest stages then the soul sings, not in plaintive regretful strain, but birdlike from an overflowing breast, with rejoicings and with mirth.

3. But the time soon arrives when the soul recognizes that life means something more than mere existence, something more than mere enjoyment, something more even than mere happiness; the time soon arrives when the soul recognizes that by the side of the Prince of Light there also dwells the Prince of Darkness; that not only is there in the Universe a great God the Good, but also a great Devil the Evil; and with the impetuosity and impassionateness of youth it gives itself up to lamentation, to indignation. The heart of the poet, the singer, is now filled with woe; he departs and leaves behind him only the lamenter, the reproacher,

the rebel. Job succeeds Miriam, Æschylus succeeds Homer, Racine and Corneille take the place of the troubadours, and Byron succeeds Shakespeare. This is the stage of fruitless lamentation and protest.

4. But unlike the bear in winter, the soul cannot feed long on its own flesh, and the time soon comes when it beholds the wasteful restlessness of mere indignation, of mere protest. It sees that to overcome the ill it must go forth manfully and do battle, and attack the enemy in his most vulnerable spots, instead of fruitlessly railing against him. Literature then becomes full of purpose; becomes aggressive, attacks now the throne, now the church, now the law, now the institution, now the person. Tragedy is followed by comedy, sentiment by satire; Æschylus is followed by Aristophanes, Horace is followed by Juvenal and Martial; Racine is followed by Voltaire, and Byron by Dickens. This is the stage of war.

5. But neither is it given unto the soul to remain long in hatred, for hatred is the child of Darkness; the goal of the soul is Love,

since Love is the child of Light. And the spirit of man soon discovers that the powers of darkness are not to be conquered by violence, by battle against the men possessed of them, but by faith in the final triumph of the Good, by submission to Fate, by endurance of what can be ·borne, by reverence towards God, and lastly by mercy towards men. The soul thus discovers its true haven ; it lays down the sword ; its voice calls no longer to strife, but to peace ; it now inspires and uplifts, and Greek literature ends with Socrates and Plato, Rome with Marcus Aurelius and Seneca, England with Carlyle and Ruskin, America with Emerson, and Germany with Goethe. Letters indeed go on in England, in America, and in Germany, but the cycle is completed ; and higher than Plato, Marcus Aurelius, Goethe, Emerson, Carlyle, and Ruskin, the soul need not seek to rise. Whatever comes henceforth can add naught new to its life ; the tones may indeed vary, but the strain must remain the same.

6. The eye of the body never indeed beholds the perfect circle ; however accurately

the hand draw, the magnifying glass quickly
reveals zigs and zags in the outline. Only
unto the eye of the spirit it is given to behold
things in their perfection, and the soul knows
that there does exist a perfect circle, magnifying glass or no magnifying glass. So history shows indeed many an irregularity in the
law just laid down for the development of the
soul, but the law is still there in its perfection, and Russian literature furnishes the best
illustration of this law. Every literature has
to go through these four stages, but nowhere
have they been passed with such regularity
as in Russia. Accordingly we have in due
order of time Pushkin the singer, Gogol the
protester, Turgenef the warrior, who .on the
very threshold of his literary career vows the
oath of a Hannibal not to rest until serfdom
and autocracy are abolished, and lastly we
have Tolstoy the preacher, the inspirer.

7. How this law has operated on Russian
soil, in Russian hearts, is the purpose of these
lectures to show. For while the laws of the
spirit are ever the same in essence, the character of their manifestation varies with time

and place, just as in Nature the same force appears in the firmament as gravitation when it binds star unto star, as attraction when it binds in the molecule atom unto atom, and in man as love when it binds heart unto heart. The phenomena therefore, natural to all literature, we shall also find here, but modified by the peculiar character of the people.

8. And the first characteristic of the Russian spirit is that it has no *originating* force. In the economy of the Aryan household, of which the Slavic race is but a member, each member has hitherto had a special office in the discharge of which its originating force was to be spent. The German has thus done the thinking of the race, the American by his inventive faculty has done the physical comforting of the race, the Frenchman the refining of the race, the Englishman the trading of the race; but the Russian has no such force peculiar to him. The office of the Slavonic race has hitherto been passive, and its highest distinction has hitherto been solely either to serve as a sieve through which the vivifying waters of European thought shall

pour upon the sleeping body of Asia, or as a dead wall to stem the wild devastating flow of Asiatic barbarism upon European civilization. The virtue of the Slavonic race is thus first of all passivity ; and as the virtue of a pipe is to be smooth and hollow, so the virtue of the Russian is first of all passive receptivity.

9. Look not therefore for creative originality in Russian literature. There is not a single form of literary development that is native to the Russian soil, not a single contribution to philosophy, to art, to letters, the form of which can be said to have been born on Russian soil. Its literary forms, like its civilization (or that which passes for its civilization), have been borrowed bodily from the west. But as action and reaction are always equal, so this very limitation of the Russian national character has been the source of many virtues of spiritual life, which Europe and America might well learn to acquire, all the more now when western thought has matured to such ripeness as to be nigh decay.

10. And herein you have the explanation of the powerful hold Russian literature has

suddenly gained upon thoughtful hearts.
Wiseacres, marvelling at the meaning of the
outburst of enthusiasm for Russian literature,
mutter "fashionable craze," and henceforth
rest content. But, O my friends, believe it
not. Craze will go as craze has come, but the
permanent force in Russian literature which
now stirs the hearts of men is not to be dis-
posed of by gossip at tea-table. Fashion can
hug a corpse for a while, and proclaim its
ghastly pallor to be delicacy of complexion,
and the icy touch of its hand to be reserved
culture, but it cannot breathe the breath of
Life into what is dead. And the present enthusiasm is kept awake, rest assured, not because of fashion, but in spite of it. Craze
will surely go, but with it will not go that
which appeals in Russian literature to all
earnest souls, because of its permanent elements over which fashion has no control.

11. For the Russians have elements in their
writings quite notable in themselves at all
times, but more notable now when letters
everywhere else seem to run to waste and
ruin, — elements without which all writing

must become in due course of time so much blacking of paper, and all speech only so much empty sound; elements without which all writing is sent off, not weighted in one corner, that it may, like unto the toy, after never so much swaying to and fro, still find its upright equilibrium, but rather like unto the sky-rocket, sent up into empty space whizzing and crackling, to end in due time in total explosion and darkness.

12. And of these elements the first is Intensity. What the Russian lacks in originality he makes up in strength; what he lacks in breadth he makes up in depth. The Russian is nothing if not intense. When he loves, he loves with all his heart; when he adores, he adores with all his soul; when he submits, he submits with all his being; when he rebels, he rebels with all his force. When Peter decides to introduce western civilization into his empire, it must be done in a day and throughout the country at once; and if human nature does not yield quickly enough to the order for change from above, soldiers must march about the streets with shears in

their hands to cut off the forbidden beard
and long coat. When tyrant Paul dies by
the hands of assassins, a scene of joy at the
deliverance takes place which is only possible on Russian streets : strangers fly into
each other's arms, embrace, kiss each other,
amid gratulations for the relief. When the
foreign invader is to be repelled, no sacrifice
is too great for the Russian ; and he does
not shrink even from setting fire to his own
Mecca, the beloved mother Moscow. When
Alexander II. undertakes to liberate Russia,
he crowds all reforms upon it at once, —
emancipation of serfs, trial by jury, local self-
government, popular education. And when
an autocratic reaction arrives, it comes with
the same storm-like rapidity and ubiquity.
From a free country Russia is changed in
one night, through the pistol-shot of a Kara-
kozof, into a despotic country, just as if some
Herman had waved his magic wand, and with
his " presto, change," had conjured up the
dead autocracy into life again. When finally
aristocratic youth is fired with the noble desire to help the ignorant peasant, home, fam-

ily, station, fortune, career, all is forsaken, and youth goes forth to live with peasant, like peasant, that it may the better instruct him. This intensity which thus permeates all life of Russia is likewise visible in its literature; but while in practical life titan-esqueness is a drawback, in literature, which is the nation's ideal life, it finds its most fruit-ful field. Hençe the Russian writer may oft, indeed, be mistaken, frequently even totally wrong, but he is never uninteresting, because always powerful.

13. In times when feebleness has become so feeble as even to invent a theory, making thinness of voice, weakness of stamina, and general emasculation literary virtues; when intellect can find adequate interest only in the chess-puzzles of a Browning, and the sense of humor can find adequate sustenance only in the table-leaping antics of a Mark Twain, and the conscience can be goaded into re-morse only by the sight of actual starvation, it is well to turn to these Russians and learn that one of the secrets of their overwhelming power is their intensity.

14. Gogol, for instance, never sets you laughing explosively. Such laughter is only on the surface ; but you can hardly read a page of his without feeling a general sense of mirth suffused as it were through every limb, and the cheek can laugh no more than the spinal column. So, too, Turgenef never sets you a weeping, but the sadness he feels he sends from his pages, circulating through your blood, and while the eye will not indeed drop a tear, for such grief is likewise mostly on the surface, the breast will heave a sigh. And Tolstoy never fires you to go forth and do a particularly good deed ; he never, like Schiller, sends you off to embrace your friend, but on laying down his book you feel a general discontent with yourself, and a longing for a nobler life than yours is takes possession of the soul.

15. This is the result of the all-absorbing, all-devouring native intensity of the Russian spirit.

16. And this intensity accounts for the suddenness with which the Russian spirit has blazed forth on the horizon, so that the succes-

sive stages of development are scarcely visible. The darkness which overcast the letters of Russia before Pushkin disappears not slowly, but the sky is lighted up suddenly by innumerable lights. Stars of the first magnitude stud it, now here, now there, until the bewildered observer beholds not twinkling points but shining luminaries. In scarcely half a century Russia has brought forth Pushkin, Lermontof, Gogol, Dostoyefsky, Turgenef, Tolstoy; and as the institutions of Western Europe became russified by the mere wave of an imperial hand, so Russian literature became modernized as if by the wave of a magic wand.

17. This national characteristic of intensity gives Russian literature a hot-house aspect. Its atmosphere is not only fragrant, but oppressively fragrant; and as in America after the civil war generals and colonels were almost too numerous for social comfort, so in Russia great authors are in well-nigh painful abundance, and the student is embarrassed not with the difficulty of selecting from the midst of poverty, but with the difficulty of

selecting from the midst of riches. And not only is its aspect that of a hot-house, but its very character has been affected. Such is the intensity of the national spirit of Russia, that it can do well but one thing at a time, and all its strength can go into only one literary form at a time. From 1800 to 1835 Russian literature is like a field on a midsummer evening, full of all manner of musical sound, and whatever hath articulate voice does nothing but sing. Batushkof sings, Pushkin sings, Lermontof sings, Koltsof sings, Turgenef versifies, and Zhukofsky, like our own poetasters, balances himself acrobatically in metrical stanzas; and where the gift of song is wanting, it shrieks and screeches, but always, observe, in well-balanced rhymes. Then comes the era of the thick periodicals, and whatever is gifted in Russia, for a time speaks only through them; lastly comes realism with an intensity unparalleled elsewhere, and everybody writes in prose, and only one kind of prose at that, — fiction. Not a drama, not a history, not an essay, not a philosophical treatise has yet grown on Russian soil; all the energy of Russia has gone into fiction, and Russia is not the country to produce, when it does produce masters, only one at a time.

18. But the great danger of intensity is extravagance; and Napoleon, who knew men well, could with justice say that the roots of Genius and Insanity are in the same tree, and indeed few are the writers of genius who have successfully coped with extravagance. It is the peculiar fortune however of the Russian writers to be comparatively free from it; and their second great virtue is the one which formed the cardinal virtue of a nation from whom we have still much to learn, the Temperance of the Greeks.

19. And of the virtues of which Temperance, Measuredness, is the parent, there are two, of which the first is Moderation and the second is Modesty : moderation with reference to things outside of the soul; modesty with reference to things inside of the soul. And for the highest example of moderation, you must read Turgenef's account of Nezhdanof's suicide in "Virgin Soil," or his account of

the drowning of Marya Pavlovna in " Back Woods ; " the first of which I will take the liberty to read to you.

" Nezhdanof sprang up from the sofa ; he went twice round the room, then stopped short for a minute lost in thought ; suddenly he shook himself, took off his " masquerading " dress, kicked it into the corner, fetched and put on his former clothes.

" Then he went up to the three-legged small table and took from the drawer two sealed envelopes, and a small object which he put into his pocket, but the envelopes he left on the table.

" He then leaned down and opened the door of the stove. . . . The stove contained a heap of ashes. This was all that was left of Nezhdanof's papers and private book of verses. . . . He had burned them all during the night. But in this same stove, leaning against one of the walls, was Marianne's portrait, Markelof's gift. Evidently Nezhdanof had not had the courage to burn this portrait with the rest ; he took it out carefully and put it on the table by the side of the sealed papers.

" Then with a determined movement of the hand he seized his cap and started for the door . . . but he stopped, came back, and went into Marianne's chamber.

" After standing motionless for a moment, he

cast a look about him, and approaching the young girl's narrow small bed — he bent down and with one suppressed sob he placed his lips, not on the pillow, but on the foot of the bed. . . . Then he stood up straight, drew his cap over his forehead, and flung himself from the room.

"Without meeting any one either in the entry, or on the staircase, or down below, he slipped out into the little enclosure. The day was cloudy, the sky lowering ; a little damp breeze bent the tops of the grass-blades and gently waved the leaves on the trees. The mill rattled and buzzed less than usual at this hour ; an odor of charcoal, of tar, and of soot came from the yard.

"Nezhdanof cast around him a scrutinizing, distrustful glance, then he walked up to the old apple-tree which had attracted his attention on the day of his arrival, when he first looked out of his chamber window. The trunk of this apple-tree was covered with dry moss, its bare and knotty branches, with but a few little green and brown leaves, stuck out here and there, raised themselves crookedly towards the heavens, like the suppliant arms of an old man, with bent elbows. Nezhdanof stood firmly on the dark earth which surrounded the foot of the apple-tree, and drew from his pocket the small object which he had previously taken from the

table drawer. — Then he looked attentively at
the windows of the little wing.

"'If some one should see me at this moment,'
he thought, 'perhaps I should put off —'

"But nowhere was a single human face to
be seen. . . . Everything seemed dead, everything turned itself away from him, drawing itself
away from him forever, leaving him alone to
the mercy of fate.   Only the factory was sending forth its rank odor, its dull uproar, and a
cold rain began to fall in fine drops, pricking
like needles.

"Then Nezhdanof looked up, through the
twisted branches of the tree beneath which he
was standing, at the gray, heavy, wet, indifferent,
blind sky; he gaped, shrugged his shoulders,
and said to himself, 'After all there is nothing
else I can do. I cannot return to Petersburg,
to prison.' He threw down his cap, and with
the premature feeling of a kind of agonizing,
not wholly unpleasant yet powerful tension of
the nerves, he put the mouth of the revolver
against his breast and pulled the trigger. . . .

"Something gave him a sudden blow not even
a very hard one . . . but already he lay on his
back, trying to make out what had happened
and how it came that he had just seen Tatyana.
. . . He wished to call to her and say, 'Oh,
there is something not right;' but already he is
speechless, and over his face into his eyes, over

his forehead into his brain, there rushes a whirl-wind of green smoke, and a flat something oppressively heavy crushed him forever to the ground.

"Nezhdanof was not mistaken in supposing he saw Tatyana ; just as he pulled the trigger, she came to one of the windows of the little wing and descried him beneath the apple-tree. She had scarcely time to ask herself, 'What is he doing under the apple-tree bareheaded in such weather as this?' when he fell backward like a sheaf of wheat ; but she felt at once that something tragic had happened ; and she rushed downstairs, out into the enclosure. . . . She ran up to Nezhdanof. . . . 'Alexis Dimitritsh, what is the matter?' But darkness had already come over him. Tatyana stooped over him, and saw blood. . . .

"'Paul!' she shouted in a strange voice, 'Paul!'

"In a few moments Marianne, Solomin, Paul, and two factory workmen were already in the enclosure ; Nezhdanof was at once raised, carried into his chamber, and placed on a sofa where he had spent his last night.

"He lay on his back, his half-closed eyes remained fixed, his face was lead-colored ; he breathed slowly and laboriously, catching each breath as if choking. Life had not yet left him.

"Marianne and Solomin stood on each side of the couch, almost as pale as Nezhdanof himself. Both were stunned, startled, crushed, especially Marianne, but they were not surprised. ' Why did not we foresee this ?' each thought ; and yet at the same time it seemed to them that they . . . yes, they had foreseen it. When he said to Marianne, ' Whatever I do, I warn you of it beforehand, you will not be surprised,' and again, when he had spoken of the two men that existed in him, who can yet not live together, did not something like a presentiment stir in her ? Why then did she not stop at that moment and reflect upon these words and this presentiment ? Why does not she dare now to look at Solomin, as if he were her accomplice . . . as if he too were suffering remorse ? Why was the feeling of infinite pity, of desperate regret with which Nezhdanof inspired her mingled with a kind of terror, with shame, with remorse ? Might she perhaps have saved him ? Why does neither of them dare to utter a word ? They hardly dare to breathe ; they wait ; what are they waiting for, Great God ?

"Solomin sent for a surgeon, although there was of course no hope ; upon the small black bloodless wound Tatyana had put a sponge with cold water, and moistened his hair also with cold water and vinegar ; suddenly Nezhdanof ceased choking and made a slight movement.

"'He is coming to himself,' muttered Solomin.

"Marianne knelt beside the sofa. . . . Nezhdanof looked at her . . . up to this moment his eyes had been fixed, like those of every dying person.

"'Ah! I am still . . . alive,' he said with a hardly audible voice. 'Unsuccessful as ever. . . . I am detaining you.'

"'Aliosha,' Marianne contrived to groan out.

"'Yes . . . soon. . . . You remember, Marianne, in my . . . poem . . . " Surround me with flowers." . . . Where then are the flowers? . . . But you are here instead . . . there, in my letter. . . .' Suddenly he began to shiver from head to foot.

"'Ah, here she is. . . . Give . . . each other . . . your hands — in my presence. . . . Quick . . . give —'

"Solomin raised Marianne's hand, her head lay on the sofa, face down, close to the very wound. As for Solomin, he stood straight and rigid, black as night.

"'So, that is right . . . so.'

"Nezhdanof began to gasp again, but this time in an entirely strange way; his chest rose and his sides contracted . . . he made evident efforts to place his hand on their clasped hands, but *his* were already dead.

"'He is going,' murmured Tatyana, who was

standing near the door; and she began to cross herself. The sobbing breaths became rarer, shorter; he was still seeking Marianne with his look, but a kind of threatening milky whiteness already veiled his eyes from within.

" 'Good! . . .' this was his last word.

" He now was no longer, but the hands of Solomin and Marianne were still joined across his breast."

20. From this pure melancholy and measured sadness, go to Dickens and read his account of the death of little Nell, or to George Eliot and read her account of Maggie Tulliver's death. I venture to think you will need no comment of mine to perceive the difference; and the difference, I regret to say, is not in favor of the English masters.

21. But not only in the field of pathos is this moderation of the Russian striking; in the field of description of nature, of which both the English and the Russian are so fond in their literature, the two literatures offer abundant material for comparison, and I will permit myself to quote to you a passage from Dickens for the purpose of illustrating how the Russians go to work with a similar subject :

"It was small tyranny for a respectable wind to go wreaking its vengeance on such poor creatures as the fallen leaves; but this wind happening to come up with a great heap of them just after venting its humor on the insulted Dragon, did so disperse and scatter them that they fled away, pell-mell, some here, some there, rolling over each other, whirling round and round upon their thin edges, taking frantic flights into the air, and playing all manner of gambols in the extremity of their distresses. Nor was this enough for its malicious fury, for not content with driving them abroad, it charged small parties of them and hunted them into the wheelwright's saw-pit and below the planks and timbers in the yard, and scattering the sawdust in the air, it looked for them underneath, and when it did meet with any, whew! how it drove them on and followed at their heels!

"The scared leaves only flew the faster for all this, and a giddy chase it was; for they got into unfrequented places, where there was no outlet, and where their pursuer kept them eddying round at his pleasure, and they crept under the eaves of the houses, and clung tightly to the sides of hay-ricks, like bats, and tore in at open chamber windows, and cowered close to hedges, and, in short, went everywhere for safety." — *Martin Chuzzlewit*, ii.

22. Of which passage the principal vice is that it does not describe to you the wind, the thing Dickens really saw, but only what Dickens thought he saw. He gives you not the original but a translation, and a translation, as you will presently see, far from faithful; he gives you not the scene, but the effect of the scene on his mind; and as Dickens started out to produce not a faithful picture, but a startling emotion, his scene is accordingly gaudy, theatrical, false. For observe, the wind is a respectable wind, and yet afflicted with pettiness of tyranny, and it wreaks vengeance; and this vengeance-wreaking wind does not come up flying, as you would expect of a wind, but it *happens* to come up leisurely, evidently taking an after-dinner stroll, as is becoming a respectable wind, which finds it not inconsistent with respectability to be vengeance-wreaking. And this respectable wind, without any motive, suddenly transforms himself into a malicious wind. Observe, he is no longer revengeful, for revenge implies something wicked done to the wind, which rouses him, while malice has no such excuse, for malice acts without cause, except from native depravity, while revenge acts always with cause. And this upright, leisurely strolling wind, now vengeance-wreaking, now malicious, again without sufficient cause changes his erect posture and kneels down, bends his head under the timbers, and the wind becomes a — peeper !

23. A conception like this may be very fine, it may be very poetic, and even very dramatic, but it is not true, for Dickens never *saw* the wind thus, else his metaphors would have been less mixed. What we see truly with our imagination we see clearly, and the metaphors born of clear sight are ever pure. Hence such description is extravagant because untrue ; hence such description is demoralizing because extravagant, immoderate.

And now read Tolstoy's description of a storm during a coach-ride : —

" It was still ten versts to the nearest station ; but the great, dark, purple cloud which had collected, God knows whence, without the smallest breeze, was movi█████wiftly upon us. The sun, which is not yet ████h by the clouds, brightly il-

lumines its dark form, and the gray streaks which
extend from it to the very horizon. From time
to time, the lightning flashes in the distance; and
a faint, dull roar is audible, which gradually increases in volume, approaches, and changes into
broken peals which embrace the whole heavens.
Vasili stands upon the box, and raises the cover
of the britchka. The coachmen put on their
armyaks, and, at every clap of thunder, remove
their hats and cross themselves. The horses
prick up their ears, puff out their nostrils as if
smelling the fresh air which is wafted from the
approaching thunder-cloud, and the britchka
rolls faster along the dusty road. I feel oppressed, and am conscious that the blood
courses more rapidly through my veins. But
the advance guard of the clouds already begins
to conceal the sun; now it has peeped forth for
the last time, has illumined the terribly dark
portion of the horizon, and vanished. The entire landscape suddenly undergoes a change, and
assumes a gloomy character. The ash woods
quiver; the leaves take on a kind of dull whit-
ish hue, and stand out against the purple background of cloud, and rustle and flutter; the
crowns of the great birches begin to rock, and
tufts of dry grass fly across the road. The
water and white-breasted swallows circle about
the britchka, and fly beneath the horses, as
though with the intention of stopping us; daws

with ruffled wings fly sideways to the wind : the edges of the leather apron, which we have buttoned up, begin to rise, and admit bursts of moist wind, and flap and beat against the body of the carriage. The lightning seems to flash in the britchka itself, dazzles the vision, and for a moment lights up the gray cloth, the border gimp, and Volodya's figure cowering in a corner. At the same moment, directly above our heads, a majestic roar resounds, which seems to rise ever higher and higher, and to spread ever wider and wider, in a vast spiral, gradually gaining force, until it passes into a deafening crash, which causes one to tremble and hold one's breath involuntarily. The wrath of God! how much poetry there is in this conception of the common people !

"The wheels whirl faster and faster. From the backs of Vasili and Philip, who is flourishing his reins, I perceive that they are afraid. The britchka rolls swiftly down the hill, and thunders over the bridge of planks. I am afraid to move, and momentarily await our universal destruction.

"Tpru! the trace is broken, and in spite of the unceasing, deafening claps of thunder, we are forced to halt upon the bridge.

"I lean my head against the side of the britchka, and, catching my breath with a sinking of the heart, I listen despairingly to the movements of Philip's fat black fingers, as he slowly ties a knot, and straightens out the traces, and strikes the side horse with palm and whip-handle.

"The uneasy feelings of sadness and terror increase within me with the force of the storm; but when the grand moment of silence arrives, which generally precedes the thunder-clap, these feelings had reached such a point, that, if this state of things had lasted a quarter of an hour, I am convinced that I should have died of excitement. At the same moment, there appears from beneath the bridge a human form, clothed in a dirty, ragged shirt, with a bloated senseless face, a shaven, wagging, totally uncovered head, crooked, nerveless legs, and a shining red stump in place of a hand, which he thrusts out directly at the britchka.

"'Ba-a-schka!'[1] Help-a-cripple-for-Christ's-sake!' says the beggar, beginning to repeat his petition by rote, in a weak voice, as he crosses himself at every word, and bows to his very belt.

"I cannot describe the feeling of chill terror which took possession of my soul at that moment. A shudder ran through my hair, and my eyes were riveted on the beggar, in a stupor of fright.

"Vasili, who bestows the alms on the jour-

[1] Imperfect pronunciation of *batiuschka*, "little father."

ney, is giving Philip directions how to strengthen
the trace ; and it is only when all is ready, and
Philip, gathering up the reins, climbs upon the
box, that he begins to draw something from his
side pocket. But we have no sooner started
than a dazzling flash of lightning, which fills the
whole ravine for a moment with its fiery glare,
brings the horses to a stand, and is accom-
panied, without the slightest interval, by such
a deafening clap of thunder that it seems as
though the whole vault of heaven were falling in ruins upon us. The wind increases ;
the manes and tails of the horses, Vasili's
cloak, and the edges of the apron, take one
direction, and flutter wildly in the bursts of the
raging gale. A great drop of rain fell heavily
upon the leather hood of the britchka, then a
second, a third, a fourth ; and all at once it beat
upon us like a drum, and the whole landscape
resounded with the regular murmur of falling
rain. I perceive, from the movement of Vasili's
elbow, that he is untying his purse; the beggar,
still crossing himself and bowing, runs close to
the wheel, so that it seems as if he would be
crushed. ' Give-for-Christ's-sake ! ' At last a
copper groschen flies past us, and the wretched
creature halts with surprise in the middle of the
road ; his smock, wet through and through, and
clinging to his lean limbs, flutters in the gale,
and he disappears from our sight.

" The slanting rain, driving before a strong wind, poured down as from a bucket; streams trickled from Vasili's frieze back into the puddle of dirty water which had collected on the apron. The dust, which at first had been beaten into pellets, was converted into liquid mud, through which the wheels splashed ; the jolts became fewer, and turbid brooks flowed in the ruts. The lightning-flashes grew broader and paler; the thunder-claps were no longer so startling after the uniform sound of the rain.

" Now the rain grows less violent; the thunder-cloud begins to disperse; light appears in the place where the sun should be, and a scrap of clear azure is almost visible through the grayish-white edges of the cloud. A moment more, and a timid ray of sunlight gleams in the pools along the road, upon the sheets of fine, perpendicular rain which fall as if through a sieve, and upon the shining, newly washed verdure of the wayside grass.

" The black thunder-cloud overspreads the opposite portion of the sky in equally threatening fashion, but I no longer fear it. I experience an inexpressibly joyous feeling of hope in life, which has quickly taken the place of my oppressive sensation of fear. My soul smiles, like Nature, refreshed and enlivened."

24. And for modesty, too, the literatures of England and Russia furnish instructive com-

parisons. Russia has no autobiographies of note. Men there were too busy with their art to have much time left to think of themselves. Turgenef writes Reminiscences, but only of others, and not of himself; and when he speaks of his own past, it is only incidentally, and with the delicacy of a maiden. Tolstoy gives, indeed, an autobiography as sincere as Rousseau's and as earnest as Mill's, but only because he believes that an account of the spiritual struggles *he* went through would be helpful to other strugglers with the terrible problems of life. But of their *personal* history there is seldom more than a trace found. Compare with this the autobiographies of Gibbon, Leigh Hunt, Mill, or even the Reminiscences of Carlyle, and the widely-branching outpourings of Ruskin in his autobiographical sketches. Not that the English over-estimate their own worth and importance, but the Russians seem to have the instinctive sense of measure in personal matters.

25. Much of this purity of taste is due to a singular circumstance in its literary history. Unlike other countries, in Russia, for a long

time, literature has been the favorite solely
of the educated and wealthy classes. Almost
all the great names of Russian literature, Pushkin, Lermontof, Hertzen, Turgenef, Zhukofsky, Griboyedof, Karamzin, Tolstoy, were aristocrats, if not always by birth, at least by surroundings. The men of letters sprung from
the people, nourished by the people, living
among the people, the Burnses, the Bérangers,
the Heines are unknown in Russia. I have
already stated that originality must not be
looked for on Russian soil; that Russian
literature is essentially an imitative literature
in its forms, hence imitative force must have
time to look about, examine, copy, and for
this leisure, wealth is necessary.

26. This absence of originality has thus
proved a source of blessing to Russian literature which well-nigh makes up the loss. For
literature thus being in the hands of men of
leisure, free from the struggle for bread, was
never governed in Russia by the law of supply and demand, and the dollar never became,
as with us, the potent, even though the tempo-
rary arbiter of its destinies. Hence the singular

purity of Russian literature in point of style. Dickens needs the dollars, and he therefore spins out his satires to a length of distance to be traversed only by seven-league boots, and in verbosity is equalled only by Thackeray. Gogol, however, not only compresses his chapters, but even burns the whole second part of his masterpiece, " Dead Souls," as unworthy of his best art. George Eliot, writing for a standard which requires three volumes for each novel, must fill her story with all manner of description which does not describe, and reflection which does not reflect; but Turgenef files and files until he is reproached more for omitting too much than for adding too much. And America's greatest living writer (I say greatest, because he is purest in spirit, gentlest in heart, and freest in mind) can still go on from year to year producing one novel annually with the regularity of a baker's muffin at breakfast. Compare with this his own master, Tolstoy, who for months forsakes his masterpiece, "Anna Karenina," because of a fastidious taste ! Hence the question why Mrs. Astor never

invites to her table literary men, which agi-
tated them recently, could not have even been
asked in Russia. Such a question is only
possible in a country where the first question
a publisher puts of a book is not whether
it is good, but whether it is likely to pay.

27. Faithfulness of labor and finish of form
are therefore characteristic of whatever has
any reputation in Russia ; and as works of art,
there are few works of the Russian masters
that are not veritable masterpieces. I say
this with confidence of Turgenef, Tolstoy,
Gogol, and Pushkin ; but I think this remark
would hold even of the lesser lights of Russian literature. A sincerity, a truthfulness, a
realness, is thus found in Russian literature,
which makes it *be* a thing of beauty instead
of doing some deeds of beauty. On reading
"Uncle Tom's Cabin," you involuntarily ask,
"What effect has this book had on slavery
in America?" On reading Turgenef's Memoirs of a Sportsman, though it accomplished
as much for the serf, you no longer ask, "What
has the book done for the serf?" You do
not think of the serf any more now that he

has ceased to be. But you do think of the innumerable things of beauty that roll out from his pages before you as if from a kaleidoscope. And if to be is greater than to do, then Russian literature is truly original, even though its forms be borrowed; since instead of seeming it *is*, and whatever truly *is*, is original.

28. From this sincerity of Russian writers comes the third great virtue of Russian literature, a virtue possessed as yet by other literatures in but a small degree. The Russian writer is first of all in earnest, and he has no time to give to *mere* entertainment, mere amusement. The Goldsmiths with their Bees and their Citizens of the World, the Addisons with their Spectators, nobly writ though these be, yet written mostly with no higher purpose than to make the breakfast-roll glide down the throat more softly, — these exist not in Russia. Things of beauty, things of entertainment, like Addison's Essays, are indeed found in Russia; but not for entertainment alone were these writ, hence not in the strain of mirth. Rather are they writ with

the blood of the heart; for to the Russian,
" Life is real, life is earnest," not a mere pas-
time, and it was given to a Russian painter
to make the all-known but singularly-forgotten
observation that Christ never — laughed !

29. But while the native endowment of
the soul, its spiritual capital, is the chief guide
of the fate of literature, other forces also affect its course, the chief among which is the
political government of the people.   In most
countries the influence of government upon
literature has been slight. Shakespeare's plays,
Milton's Paradise, were not affected by the
political struggles of England.   The sole
writing of Milton which was affected by English politics, his prose, belongs to literature
only in so far as it throws light on the author
of Paradise Lost.   Dante's Divine Comedy,
charged though it be with the political elec-
tricity of his times, was but little affected by
the state of government.   In other countries
the government of the people was as much
itself an effect of the native endowment of
the soul as its literature ; and government and
literature flowed therefore side by side, in two

parallel streams, seldom interfering with each other's course. In Russia, however, government has extended a powerful influence on literature, and the most marked effect of its influence is the short-livedness of most Russian authors. The calm, peaceful existence of the literary man has already been sung by Carlyle as a life-lengthener. In Russia, however, the same fatality which has pursued its political rulers has also pursued its spiritual rulers; and as most conquerors have died an unnatural death, so most writers have died an unnatural death, or only after an unnatural life. The witticism of Mark Twain, that the bed must be a most fatal place, since most people die in bed, is not applicable to Russian emperors and Russian writers. Few of them can be said to have died in their beds. Griboyedof is assassinated; Pushkin and Lermontof are murdered; Gogol is found dead from bodily starvation, and Byelinsky is found dead from spiritual starvation; Batushkof dies insane; Dostoyefsky and Chernishefsky are in prison the best years of their lives; Turgenef can find the length of his days only in exile,

and Tolstoy the length of his in ploughing
fields.   For such a strange disharmony in the
lives of Russian men of letters, the government is largely responsible.   An autocracy
which feels itself called to wrap literature
tightly in swaddling-clothes, and establishes a
censorship which does not shrink even from
making verbal changes in the works of the artist to improve his style, can accomplish little
more than the shortening of literary lives.
For literature is a flower which can only wither
at the touch of unhallowed hands, and the
rude hands of the censor are far from being
hallowed.

30. Hence Russian literature not only *is*
a mere fragment, a mere brick of the vast
edifice which it is capable of becoming; it
is even bound to remain a mere fragment for
a long time to come.   For as Socrates lived
in Plato, Plato in Aristotle, and Aristotle in
the Schoolmen, as Lessing lived in Goethe,
Goethe in Heine, and Heine in young Germany, so great literary fathers reappear in the
progeny of the next generation; the reproduction is indeed oft puny enough, still the

reproduction is there. But in Russia, while Pushkin lived in Gogol, and Gogol in Turgenef, the generation which was to inherit the kingdom left by Turgenef and Tolstoy is now buried in fortresses and dungeons. And as in America mammon has so eaten away literary aspiration as to leave Emerson and Hawthorne, Prescott and Motley, intellectually childless, so in Russia, autocracy has so eaten away the literary material as to leave the great masters childless. · ·

31. Fortunately, though deprived by despotism of all power of propagation on Russian soil, the noble spirit of Russian literature has by a force I cannot but call divine been allowed to be propagated on foreign soil; and if the literature of the west, which is now stagnating in the pools of doubt, irreverence, mammon, and cold intellectualism, misnamed culture, is to be purified, the purification must come from the breath of Life which blows from Russia. This is the true meaning of the present craze for Russian authors. There is a force in them which the mass instinctively recognizes as divine; it feels for it, gropes for it,

and the Devil, as usual, is the first to seize for his purposes whatever noble impulse comes over men, and this search for the divine of the mass becomes a sham, a fashionable craze. Hence the rage, the boom. This is the inevitable stage of falsehood through which every noble aspiration must pass. By and by the stage of truth must come, and come it shall, in due time. Russian authors will then be read not because it is the fashion and the craze, but because they have a message from the very heavens to deliver unto him that hath eyes to see and ears to hear : the message of sincerity, the message of earnestness, the message of love. Then will have been reached the stage of truth.

32. Out of this crampedness of Russian literature by government developed that virtue of its masters, which with their sincerity and simplicity, or moderation, forms a most beautiful trinity of graces ; I mean their freedom. You will indeed hear full many a yard-stick critic as he goes about with his load of pigeon-holed boxes to take measure of each author, and label him, and duly relegate him

to convenient pigeon-hole, — such critic you
will hear discourse much about classicism,
and romanticism, and realism, and of their
prevalence at different times in Russian literature. Believe it not! The Russian author
who is at all worth classifying is slave of no
school; he is free, for he is a worshipper of the
truth which alone maketh men free, he is a
school unto himself. Is Gogol a realist? He
gives you indeed the reality, but he breathes
into it a beauty only visible to idealizing eyes.
Is Turgenef a realist? When thrilled with the
unspeakable beauty of the sky, he depicts it
so as to realize for you the ideal. And when
Tolstoy is thrilled with a moral emotion, he
depicts it so as to idealize the real for you.
The Russians thus refuse to be classified.
And they belong to only one class, — the
class of those that cannot be classified.

33. Thus has it come to pass that the west,
to which Russian literature owes its nourishment, is now in its old age to be nourished
by its foster child. The child is to become
the father of the man; and Russian literature
is henceforth to be the source of the regene-

ràtion of the western spirit. As the future
fighters for freedom will have to look to the
Perofskayas, to the Bardines, and the Zassul-
itshes, and to the unnamed countless victims
of the Siberian snow-fields for models of heroism, so methinks henceforth writers must look
to the Russians for models in their art: to
Gogol for pure humor, to Turgenef for the
worship of natural beauty, to Tolstoy for the
worship of moral beauty.

LECTURE II.

————•————

PUSHKIN.

1. I HAVE stated in the first lecture that I should treat of Pushkin as the singer. Pushkin has indeed done much besides singing. He has written not only lyrics and ballads but also tales: tales in prose and tales in verse; he has written novels, a drama, and even a history. He has thus roamed far and wide, still he is only a singer. And even a cursory glance at his works is enough to show the place which belongs to him. I say belongs, because the place he holds has a prominence out of proportion to the merits of the writer. Among the blind the one-eyed is king, and the one-eyed Pushkin — for the moral eye is totally lacking in this man — came when there as yet was no genuine song

in Russia, but mere noise, reverberation of sounding brass; and Pushkin was hailed as the voice of voices, because amidst the universal din his was at least clear. Of his most ambitious works, " Boris Godunof " is not a drama, with a central idea struggling in the breast of the poet for embodiment in art, but merely a series of well-painted pictures, and painted not for the soul, but only for the eye. His " Eugene Onyegin " contains many fine verses, much wit, much biting satire, much bitter scorn, but no indignation burning out of the righteous heart. His satire makes you smile, but fails to rouse you to indignation. In his " Onyegin," Pushkin often pleases you, but he never stirs you. Pushkin is in literature what the polished club-man is in society. In society the man who can repeat the most bon-mots, tell the most amusing anecdotes, and talk most fluently, holds the ear more closely than he that speaks from the heart. So Pushkin holds his place in literature because he is brilliant, because his verse is polished, his language chosen, his wit pointed, his prick stinging. But he has no aspiration, no hope ; he has none of the elements which make the writings of the truly great helpful. Pushkin, in short, has nothing to give. Since to be able to give one must have, and Pushkin was a spiritual pauper.

2. And what is true of his more sustained works, is equally true of his lesser works. They all bear the mark of having come from the surface, and not from the depths. His " Prisoner of the Caucasus," his " Fountain of Bachtshisarai," his "Gypsies," are moreover weighted down with the additional load of having been written directly under the influence of Byron. And as health is sufficient unto itself and it is only disease which is contagious, Byron, who was sick at heart himself, could only impart disease and not health. Byron moreover had besides his gift of song the element of moral indignation against corrupt surroundings. Pushkin had not even this redeeming feature.

3. Pushkin therefore is not a poet, but only a singer ; for he is not a maker, a creator. There is not a single idea any of his works can be said to stand for. His is merely a

skill. No idea circulates in his blood giving him no rest until embodied in artistic form. His is merely a skill struggling for utterance because there is more of it than he can hold. Pushkin has thus nothing to give you to carry away. All he gives is pleasure, and the pleasure he gives is not that got by the hungry from a draught 'of nourishing milk, but that got by the satiated from a draught of intoxicating wine. He is the exponent of beauty solely, without reference to an ultimate end. Gogol uses his sense of beauty and creative impulse to protest against corruption, to give vent to his moral indignation ; Turgenef uses his sense of beauty as a weapon with which to fight *his* mortal enemy, mankind's deadly foe ; and Tolstoy uses his sense of, beauty to preach the ever-needed gospel of love. But Pushkin uses his sense of beauty merely to give it expression. He sings indeed like a siren, but he sings without purpose. Hence, though he is the greatest versifier of Russia, — not poet, observe ! — he is among the least of its writers.

4. Towards the end of his early extinguished

life he showed, indeed, signs of better things.
In his " Captain's Daughter " he depicts a
heroic simplicity, the sight of which is truly
refreshing, and here Pushkin becomes truly
noble. As a thing of purity, as a thing of
calmness, as a thing of beauty, in short, the
" Captain's Daughter " stands unsurpassed·
either in Russia or out of Russia. Only
Goldsmith's " Vicar of Wakefield," Gogol's
" Taras Bulba," and the Swiss clergyman's
" Broom Merchant," can be worthily placed
by its side.   But this nobility is of the lowly,
humble kind, to be indeed thankful for as
all nobility must be, whether it be that of the
honest farmer who tills the soil in silence, or
that of the gentle Longfellow who cultivates
his modest muse in equal quietness.   But
there is the nobility of the nightingale and
the nobility of the eagle ; there is the nobility
of the lamb and the nobility of the lion ; and
beside the titanesqueness of Gogol, and Turgenef, and Tolstoy, the nobility of Pushkin,
though high enough on its own plane, is
relatively low.

5. Mere singer then that Pushkin is, he is

accordingly at his best only in his lyrics. But the essence of a lyric is music, and the essence of music is harmony, and the essence of harmony is form ; hence in beauty of form Pushkin is unsurpassed, and among singers he is peerless. His soul is a veritable Æolian harp. No sooner does the wind begin to blow than his soul is filled with music. His grace is only equalled by that of Heine, his ease by that of Goethe, and his melody by that of Tennyson. I have already said that Pushkin is not an eagle soaring in the heavens, but he is a nightingale perched singing on the tree. But this very perfection of form makes his lyrics well-nigh untranslatable, and their highest beauty can only be felt by those who can read them in the original.

6. In endeavoring therefore to present Pushkin to you, I shall present to you not the nine tenths of his works which were written only by his hands, — his dramas, his tales, his romances, whether in prose or verse, — but the one tithe of his works which was writ from his heart. For Pushkin was essentially a lyric

4

singer, and whatever comes from this side of
his being is truly original ; all else, engrafted
upon him as it is from without, either from
ambition or from imitation, cannot be called
his writing, that which he alone and none
others had to deliver himself of.   What
· message Pushkin had to deliver at all to
his fellow-men is therefore found in his
lyrics.

7. Before proceeding, however, to·look at
this singer Pushkin, it is necessary to establish
a standard by which his attainment is to be
judged.   And that we may ascertain how
closely Pushkin approaches the highest, I
venture to read to you the following poem,
as the highest flight which the human soul
is capable of taking heavenward on the wings
of song.

HYMN TO FORCE.

BY WM. R. THAYER.

I AM eternal !
I throb through the ages ;
I am the Master
Of each of Life's stages.

I quicken the blood
Of the mate-craving lover ;
The age-frozen heart
With daisies I cover.

Down through the ether
I hurl constellations ;
Up from their earth-bed
I wake the carnations.

I laugh in the flame
As I kindle and fan it;
I crawl in the worm ;
I leap in the planet.

Forth from its cradle
I pilot the river ;
In lightning and earthquake
I flash and I quiver.

My breath is the wind;
My bosom the ocean ;
My form 's undefined ;
My essence is motion.

The braggarts of science
Would weigh and divide me ;
Their wisdom evading,
I vanish and hide me.

My glances are rays
From stars emanating;
My voice through the spheres
Is sound, undulating.

I am the monarch
Uniting all matter:
The atoms I gather;
The atoms I scatter.

I pulse with the tides —
Now hither, now thither;
I grant the tree sap;
I bid the bud wither.

I always am present,
Yet nothing can bind me;
Like thought evanescent,
They lose me who find me. ✗

8. I consider a poem of this kind (and I regret that there are very few such in any language) to stand at the very summit of poetic aspiration. For not only is it perfect in form, and is thus a thing of beauty made by the hands of man, but its subject is of the very highest, since it is a hymn, a praise of God, even though the name of the Most High be not there. For what is heaven? Heaven is

✗ *Confessions of Hermes."*

a state where the fellowship of man with man is such as to leave no room for want to the one while there is abundance to the other. Heaven is a state where the wants of the individual are so cared for that he needs the help of none. But if there be no longer any need of toiling, neither for neighbor nor for self, what is there left for the soul to do but to praise God and glorify creation? A hymn like the above, then, is the outflow of a spirit which hath a heavenly peace. And this is precisely the occupation with which the imagination endows the angels; the highest flight of the soul is therefore that in which it is so divested of the interests of the earth as to be filled only with reverence and worship. And this hymn to Force seems to me to have come from a spirit which, at the time of its writing at least, attained such freedom from the earthly.

9. Such a poem being then at one end of the scale, the highest because it gratifies the soul's highest need, on the opposite end, on the lowest, is found that which gratifies the soul's lowest need, its need for novelty, its

curiosity. And this is done by purely narrative writing, of which the following is a good example : —

THE BLACK SHAWL.

I GAZE demented on the black shawl,
And my cold soul is torn by grief.

When young I was and full of trust
I passionately loved a young Greek girl.

The charming maid, she fondled me,
But soon I lived the black day to see.

Once as were gathered my jolly guests,
A detested Jew knocked at my door.

Thou art feasting, he whispered, with friends,
But betrayed thou art by thy Greek maid.

Moneys I gave him and curses,
And called my servant, the faithful.

We went ; I flew on the wings of my steed,
And tender mercy was silent in me.

Her threshold no sooner I espied,
Dark grew my eyes, and my strength departed.

The distant chamber I enter alone —
An Armenian embraces my faithless maid.

Darkness around me: flashed the dagger;
To interrupt his kiss the wretch had no time.

And long I trampled the headless corpse, —
And silent and pale at the maid I stared.

I remember her prayers, her flowing blood,
But perished the girl, and with her my love.

The shawl I took from the head now dead,
And wiped in silence the bleeding steel.

When came the darkness of eve, my serf
Threw their bodies into the billows of the
    Danube.

Since then I kiss no charming eyes,
Since then I know no cheerful days.

I gaze demented on the black shawl,
And my cold soul is torn by grief.

10. The purpose of the author here was only to tell a story; and as success is to be measured by the ability of a writer to adapt his means to his ends, it must be acknowledged that Pushkin is here eminently successful. For the story is here well told;

well told because simply told; the narrative moves, uninterrupted by excursions into side-fields.   In its class therefore this poem must stand high, but it is of the lowest class.

11. For well told though this story be, it is after all only a story, with no higher purpose than merely to gratify curiosity, than merely to amuse. Its art has no higher purpose than to copy faithfully the event, than to be a faithful photograph; and moreover it is the story not of an emotion, but of a passion, and an ignoble passion at that; the passion is jealousy,—in itself an ugly thing, and the fruit of this ugly thing is a still uglier thing, —a murder. The subject therefore is not a thing of beauty, and methinks that the sole business of art is first of all to deal with things of beauty. Mediocrity, meanness, ugliness, are fit subjects for art only when they can be made to serve a higher purpose, just as the sole reason for tasting wormwood is the improvement of health. But this higher purpose is here wanting. Hence I place such a poem on the lowest plane of art.

THE OUTCAST.

ON a rainy autumn evening
Into desert places went a maid ;
And the secret fruit of unhappy love
In her trembling hands she held.
All was still: the woods and the hills
Asleep in the darkness of the night ;
And her searching glances
In terror about she cast.

And on this babe, the innocent,
Her glance she paused with a sigh:
"Asleep thou art, my child, my grief,
Thou knowest not my sadness.
Thine eyes will ope, and though with longing,
To my breast shalt no more cling.
No kiss for thee to-morrow
From thine unhappy mother.

Beckon in vain for her thou wilt,
My everlasting shame, my guilt !
Me forget thou shalt for aye,
But thee forget shall not I ;
Shelter thou shalt receive from strangers ;
Who 'll say: Thou art none of ours !
Thou wilt ask: Where are my parents ?
But for thee no kin is found.

Hapless one ! with heart filled with sorrow,
Lonely amid thy mates,

Thy spirit sullen to the end
Thou shalt behold the fondling mothers.
A lonely wanderer everywhere,
Cursing thy fate at all times,
Thou the bitter reproach shalt hear . . .
Forgive me, oh, forgive me then!

Asleep! let me then, O hapless one,
To my bosom press thee once for all;
A law unjust and terrible
Thee and me to sorrow dooms.
While the years have not yet chased
The guiltless joy of thy days,
Sleep, my darling; let no bitter griefs
Mar thy childhood's quiet life!"

But lo, behind the woods, near by,
The moon brings a hut to light.
Forlorn, pale, trembling
To the doors she came nigh;
She stooped, and gently laid down
The babe on the strange threshold.
In terror away she turned her eyes
And disappeared in the darkness of the night.

12. This also is a narrative poem; but it tells something more than a story. A new element is here added. For it not only gratifies our curiosity about the mother and the babe, but it also moves us. And it moves not

our low passion, but it stirs our high emotion. Not our anger is here roused, as against the owner of the black shawl, but our pity is stirred for the innocent babe ; and even the mother, though guilty enough, stirs our hearts. Here, too, as in the " Black Shawl," the art of the narrator is perfect. The few touches of description are given only in so far as they vivify the scene and furnish a fit background for the mother and child. But the theme is already of a higher order, and in rank I therefore place the " Outcast " one plane above the " Black Shawl."

13. The two poems I have just read you are essentially ballads ; they deal indeed with emotion, but only incidentally.   Their chief purpose is the telling of the story. I shall now read you some specimens of a higher order of poetry, — of that which reflects the pure emotion which the soul feels when beholding beauty in Nature. I consider such poetry as on a higher plane, because this emotion is at bottom a reverence before the powers of Nature, hence a worship of God.   It is at bottom a confession of the soul of its

humility before its Creator. It is the constant presence of this emotion which gives permanent value to the otherwise tame and commonplace writings of Wordsworth. Wordsworth seldom climbs the height he attains in those nine lines, the first of which are : —

> " My heart leaps up when I behold
> A rainbow in the sky."

But here Pushkin is always on the heights. And the first I will read you shall be one in which the mere sense of Nature's beauty finds vent in expression without any conscious ethical purpose. It is an address to the last cloud.

THE CLOUD.

O LAST cloud of the scattered storm,
Alone thou sailest along the azure clear ;
Alone thou bringest the darkness of shadow ;
Alone thou marrest the joy of the day.

Thou but recently hadst encircled the sky,
When sternly the lightning was winding about
　　thee.
Thou gavest forth mysterious thunder,
Thou hast watered with rain the parched earth.

Enough; hie thyself. Thy time hath passed.
The earth is refreshed, and the storm hath fled,
And the breeze, fondling the leaves of the trees,
Forth chases thee from the quieted heavens.

14. Observe, here the poet has no ultimate
end but that of giving expression to the overflowing sense of beauty which comes over the
soul as he beholds the last remnant of a thunder-storm floating off into airy nothingness.
But it is a beauty which ever since the days
of Noah and his rainbow has filled the human soul with marvelling and fearing adora-
tion.   Beautiful, then, in a most noble sense
this poem indeed is.   Still, I cannot but consider the following few lines to the Birdlet,
belonging as the poem does to the same class
with " The Cloud," as still superior.

THE BIRDLET.

God's birdlet knows
Nor care nor toil;
Nor weaves it painfully
An everlasting nest;
Through the long night on the twig it slumbers;
When rises the red sun,
To the voice of God listens birdie,
And it starts and it sings.

When spring, nature's beauty,
And the burning summer have passed,
And the fog and the rain
By the late fall are brought,
Men are wearied, men are grieved;
But birdie flies into distant lands,
Into warm climes, beyond the blue sea, —
Flies away until the spring.

15. For a poem of this class this is a veritable gem; for not only is its theme a thing of beauty, but it is a thing of tender beauty. Who is there among my hearers that can contemplate this birdlet, this wee child of God, as the poet hath contemplated it, and not feel a gentleness, a tenderness, a meltedness creep into every nook and corner of his being? But the lyric beauty of the form, and the tender emotion roused in our hearts by this poem, form by no means its greatest merit. To me the well-nigh inexpressible beauty of these lines lies in the spirit which shineth from them, — the spirit of unreserved trust in the fatherhood of God. "When fog and rain by the late fall are brought, men are wearied, men are grieved, but birdie —" My friends,

the poet has written here a commentary on
the heavenly words of Christ, which may well
be read with immeasurable profit by our wiseacres of supply-and-demand economy, and
the consequence-fearing Associated or Dis-
sociated Charity. For if I mistake not, it
was Christ that uttered the strangely un-
heeded words, " Be not anxious for the morrow. . . . Behold the birds of the heaven, that
they sow not, neither do they reap, nor gather
into barns, and your heavenly Father feedeth
them." Fine words these, to be read rever-
ently from the pulpit on Sunday, but to be
laughed at in the counting-room and in the
charity-office on Monday. But the singer
was stirred by this trustfulness of birdie, all
the more beautiful because unconscious, and
accordingly celebrates it in lines of well-nigh
unapproachable tenderness and grace !

16. There is, however, one realm of creation yet grander and nobler than that visible to the eye of the body. Higher than
the visible stands the invisible ; and when the
soul turns from the contemplation of the outward universe to the contemplation of the in-

ward universe, to the contemplation of affection and aspiration, its flight must of necessity
be higher.   Hence the high rank of those
strains of song which the soul gives forth
when stirred by affection, by love to the
children of God, whether they be addressed
by Wordsworth to a butterfly, by Burns to
a mouse, or by Byron to a friend.   You
have in English eight brief lines which for
this kind of song are a model from their
simplicity, tenderness, and depth.

LINES IN AN ALBUM.

As over the cold, sepulchral stone
Some name arrests the passer-by,
Thus when thou viewest this page alone
May mine attract thy pensive eye.

And when these lines by thee are read
Perchance in some succeeding year,
Reflect on me as on the dead,
And think my heart is buried here !

17. It is this song of love for one's kind
which makes Burns, Heine, and Goethe pre-
eminently the singers of the human heart
when it finds itself linked to one other heart.

And it is this strain which gives everlasting life
to the following breath of Pushkin's muse :

TO A FLOWER.

A FLOWERET, withered, odorless,
In a book forgot I find ;
And already strange reflection
Cometh into my mind.

Bloomed where ?   When ?   In what spring?
And how long ago ?   And plucked by whom ?
Was it by a strange hand, was it by a dear hand ?
And wherefore left thus here ?

Was it in memory of a tender meeting ?
Was it in memory of a fated parting ?
Was it in memory of a lonely walk
In the peaceful fields, or in the shady woods ?

Lives he still ? lives she still ?
And where is their nook this very day ?
Or are they too withered,
Like unto this unknown floweret ?

18. But from the love of the individual the
growing soul comes in time to the love of the
race ; or rather, we only love an individual
because he is to us the incorporation of some

Ideal. And let the virtue for which we love him once be gone, he may indeed keep our good will, but our love for him is clean gone out. This is because the soul in its ever-upward, heavenward flight alights with its love upon individuals solely in the hope of finding here its ideal, its heaven realized. But it is not given unto one person to fill the whole of a heaven-searching soul. Only the ideal, God alone, can wholly fill it. Hence the next strain to that of love for the individual is this longing for the ideal, a longing for what is so vague to most of us, a longing to which therefore not wholly inappropriately the name has been given of a longing for the Infinite.

19. And of this longing, Heine has given in eight lines immeasurably pathetic expression :

> " Ein Fichtenbaum steht einsam
> Im Norden auf kahler Höh'
> Ihn schläfert ; mit weisser Decke
> Umhüllen ihn Eis und Schnee.
> Er träumt von einer Palme,
> Die, fern im Morgenland,
> Einsam und schweigend trauert
> Auf brennender Felsenwand."

Heine has taken the evergreen pine in the cold clime, as the emblem of this longing, and a most noble emblem it is. But I cannot help feeling that in choosing a fallen angel, as Pushkin has on the same subject, he was enabled to give it a zenith-like loftiness and a nadir like depth not to be found in Heine.

THE ANGEL.

AT the gates of Eden a tender Angel
With drooping head was shining;
A demon gloomy and rebellious
Over the abyss of hell was flying.

The spirit of Denial, the spirit of Doubt,
The spirit of purity espied;
And unwittingly the warmth of tenderness
He for the first time learned to know.

Adieu, he spake. Thee I saw;
Not in vain hast thou shone before me.
Not all in the world have I hated,
Not all in the world have I scorned.

20. Hitherto we have followed Pushkin only through his unconscious song; only through

that song of which his soul was so full as to find an outlet, as it were, without any deliberate effort on his part.   But not even unto the bard is it given to remain in this childlike health.   For Nature ever works in circles. Starting from health, the soul indeed in the end arrives at health, but only through the road of disease.   And a good portion of the conscious period in the life of the soul is taken up by doubt, by despair, by disease.   Hence when the singer begins to reflect, to philosophize, his song is no longer that of health.   This is the reason why Byron and Shelley have borne so little fruit.   Their wail is the cry not of a mood, but of their whole being ; it is not the cry of health temporarily deranged, but the cry of disease. With the healthy Burns, on the other hand, his poem, " Man was made to Mourn," reflects only a stage which all growing souls must pass.   So Pushkin, too, in his growth, at last arrives at a period when he writes the following lines, not the less beautiful for being the offspring of disease, as all lamentation must needs be : —

" Whether I roam along the noisy streets,
  Whether I enter the peopled temple,
  Or whether I sit by thoughtless youth,
  My thoughts haunt me everywhere.

" I say, swiftly go the years by :
  However great our number now,
  Must all descend the eternal vaults, —
  Already struck has some one's hour.

" And if I gaze upon the lonely oak,
  I think : The patriarch of the woods
· Will survive my passing age
  As he survived my father's age.

" And if a tender babe I fondle,
  Already I mutter, Fare thee well !
  I yield my place to thee ;
  For me 't is time to decay, to bloom for thee.

" Thus every day, every year,
  With death I join my thought
  Of coming death the day,
  Seeking among them to divine

" Where will Fortune send me death, —
  In battle, in my wanderings, or on the waves ?
  Or shall the neighboring valley
  Receive my chilled dust?

" But though the unfeeling body
Can equally moulder everywhere,
I, still, my birthland nigh,
Would have my body lie.

" Let near the entrance to my grave
Cheerful youth be engaged in play,
And let indifferent creation
Shine there with beauty eternally."

21. Once passed through its mumps and
measles, the soul of the poet now becomes
conscious of its heavenly gift, and begins to
have a conscious purpose. The poet becomes moralized, and the song becomes
ethical. This is the beginning of the final
stage, which the soul, if its growth continue
healthy, must reach ; and Pushkin, when singing, does retain his health. Accordingly in his
address to the Steed, the purpose is already
clearly visible.

THE HORSE.

WHY dost thou neigh, O spirited steed ;
Why thy neck so low,
Why thy mane unshaken,
Why thy bit not gnawed ?

Do I then not fondle thee ;
Thy grain to eat art thou not free ;
Is not thy harness ornamented,
Is not thy rein of silk,
Is not thy shoe of silver,
Thy stirrup not of gold ?
The steed, in sorrow, answer gives :
Hence am I still,
Because the distant tramp I hear,
The trumpet's blow, and the arrow's whiz ;
And hence I neigh, since in the field
No longer shall I feed,
Nor in beauty live, and fondling,
Nor shine with the harness bright.
For soon the stern enemy
My harness whole shall take,
And the shoes of silver
From my light feet shall tear.
Hence it is that grieves my spirit ;
That in place of my chaprak
With thy skin shall cover he
My perspiring sides.

22. It is thus that the singer lifts up his voice against the terrors of war. It is thus that he protests against the struggle between brother and brother; and the effect of the protest is all the more potent that it is put into the mouth, not as Nekrassof puts it, of the

singer, but into that of a dumb, unreasoning beast.

23. We have now reached the last stage of the development of Pushkin's singing soul. For once conscious of a moral purpose, he cannot remain long on the plane of mere protest; this is mere negation. What is to him the truth must likewise be sung, and he utters the note of affirmation; this in his greatest poem, —

THE PROPHET.

TORMENTED by the thirst for the Spirit,
I was dragging myself in a sombre desert,
And a six-winged seraph appeared
Unto me on the parting of the roads.
With fingers as light as a dream
He touched mine eyes ;
And mine eyes opened wise,
Like unto the eyes of a frightened eagle.
He touched mine ears,
And they filled with din and ringing.
And I heard the trembling of the heavens,
And the flight of the angels' wings,
And the creeping of the polyps in the sea,
And the growth of the vine in the valley.

And he took hold of my lips,
And out he tore my sinful tongue,
With its empty and false speech.
And the fang of the wise serpent
Between my terrified lips he placed
With bloody hand.
And ope he cut my breast with a sword,
And out he took my trembling heart,
And a coal blazing with flame
He shoved into the open breast.
Like a corpse I lay in the desert ;
And the voice of the Lord called unto me :
" Arise ! O prophet and guide, and listen, —
Be thou filled with my will,
And going over land and sea,
Burn with the Word the hearts of men ! "

24. This is the highest flight of Pushkin. He knew that the poet comes to deliver the message. But *what* the message was, was not given unto him to utter. For God only speaks through those that speak for him, and Pushkin's was not yet a God-filled soul. Hence the last height left him yet to climb, the height from which the " Hymn of Force " is sung, Pushkin did not climb. Pushkin's song, in short, was so far only an utterance of a gift, it had not become as yet a part

of his life. And the highest is only attainable not when our lives are guided by our gifts, but when our gifts are guided by our lives. How this thus falling short of a natively richly endowed soul became possible, can be told only from a study of his life. To Pushkin his poetic ideal bore the same relation to his practical life that the Sunday religion of the business-man bears to his Monday life. To the ordinary business man, Christ's words are a seeing guide to be followed in church, but a blind enough guide, not to be followed on the street. Hence Pushkin's life is barren as a source of inspiration towards what life ought to be; but it is richly fruitful as a terrifying warning against what life ought not to be.

25. Pushkin died at the age of thirty-eight, at a time when he may be said to have just begun to live. Once more then we have before us a mere fragment, a mere possibility, a mere promise of what the great soul was capable of becoming, of what the great soul was perhaps destined to become. Pushkin is thus a typical example of the fate of the Slavonic soul.

And the same phases we had occasion to observe as gone through by the race, we now find here likewise gone through by the individual. It is this which makes Pushkin eminently a national singer, a Russian singer. The satire of Gogol, the synthesis of Turgenef, the analysis of Tolstoy, might have indeed flourished on any other soil. Nay, Turgenef and Tolstoy are men before they are Russians; but the strength of Pushkin as a force in Russian literature comes from this his very weakness. Pushkin is a Russian before he is a man, his song is a Russian song; hence though many have been the singers in Russia since his day, none has yet succeeded in filling his place. For many are indeed called, but few are chosen; and the chosen Russian bard was — Alexander Pushkin.

LECTURE III.

———◆———

GOGOL.

1. With the departure of the eighteenth century there also disappeared from Russia that dazzling glitter which for well-nigh half a century had blinded the eyes of Europe. Catherine was now dead, Potyomkin was dead, Suvorof was living an exile in a village, and Panin was idle on his estates. And now stripped of its coat of whitewash, autocracy stood bare in all its blackness. Instead of mother-Catherine, Paul was now ruling, and right fatherly he ruled! Such terror was inspired by this emperor, that at the sight of their father-Tsar his subjects at last began to scamper in all directions like a troop of mice at the sight of a cat. For half a decade Russia was thus held in terror, until the rule of the maniac could no longer be endured.

At last Panin originates, Pahlen organizes, and Benigsen executes a plan, the accomplishment of which finds Paul on the morrow lying in state with a purple face, and the marks of the shawl which strangled him carefully hid by a high collar. " His Majesty died of apoplexy," the populace is told. Alexander the Benign comes upon the throne, greeted, indeed, by his subjects, in the ecstasy of the delivery, like an angel, but cursed by them as a demon ere the five-and-twenty years of his rule have passed. The Holy Alliance, Shishkof and Arakcheyef, were more than even Russians could endure, and formidable protest is at last made by the armed force of the Decembrists. The protest fails ; five bodies swinging from the gallows, and a hundred exiles buried in Siberia alive, leave a monument of such failure terrible in its ghastliness even for Russian history. The iron hand of Nicholas now rests on the country, and for thirty years the autocrat can proudly say that now order reigns in Russia. Order? Yes ; but it is the order and quiet of the graveyard, the peace of death.

2. But not all is quiet. Defeated on the field of arms, the spirit of protest seeks and at last finds a battle-field where neither the trampling hoofs of horses nor the shot of cannon can avail. The spirit of man intrenches itself behind ideas, behind letters, and here it proves impregnable even against the autocracy of a Nicholas. Defeated on the field of war, the spirit of man protests in literature. The times call for the voice, and the voice is soon heard. This voice is the voice of Nicolai Gogol.

3. Gogol is the protester, the merciless critic of the weakness of autocracy. I have placed Pushkin, the greatest of Russia's singers, as among the least of its writers, because he hath no purpose. I place Gogol far above Pushkin, because Gogol is the first master of Russian literature in whom purpose is not only visible, but is also shown. Gogol's art protests not unconsciously; but the man Gogol uses the artist Gogol as a means for giving voice to the protest against what his noble soul rebels.

4. For, O my friends, I cannot emphasize

it too strongly that our gifts — whether they consist in wealth, or in the ability to sing, to paint, to build, or to count — are not given unto us to be used for our pleasure merely, or as means of our advancement, whether social or intellectual. But they are given unto us that we may use them for helping those who need help. Talk not therefore of art for its own sake ; that art needs no purpose, but is an end unto itself. Such talk is only a convenient way of evading the Heaven-imposed responsibility of *using for others* those gifts with which a merciful power hath endowed their undeserving possessors. Art, therefore, to be truly worthy, must have a purpose, and, execution being equal, that art is highest, which hath the highest purpose ; that art lowest, which hath the lowest purpose.

5. But it was not given to Gogol to announce the loftiest message, the message of peace, of love, of submission, the message of Tolstoy ; the times of Gogol were not ripe for this ; the times of Gogol called for indignation, for protest, and Gogol is the indignant protester.

6. Hitherto, whatever force has been exerted towards protesting against the misrule of Russia by autocracy has come from the South. Stenka Rasin, Pugatchef, came not from the North but from the South. And the most formidable division of the Decembrist conspirators of 1825 was that of Pestel and Muraviof, with their headquarters in the South. And even the policy of terrorizing the autocracy by assassination, which was adopted in our own day by the most formidable opponents of the government, by the revolutionists miscalled Nihilists, also originated in the South, — with Ossinsky and his comrades in Kief. Gogol, the protester in literature, was likewise a Southerner. And it will be worth while to cast a glance at this country and see what therein is to make it thus a hot-bed of protest.

7. Beyond the waterfalls of the Dnieper there extends a to the eye boundless land of prairie which for ages has been the rendezvous of all manner of wild, lawless, but sturdy folk. Of this land Gogol himself has given a description glowingly beautiful as only the

love of a Little Russian for the Steppe could give. Taras Bulba had just started out with his two sons to join the camp of the Cossaks.

" Meanwhile the steppe had already received them all into its green embrace, and the high grass surrounding them hid them, and the black Cossaks' caps alone now gleamed between its stalks.

" ' Aye, aye, fellows, what is the matter ; why so quiet?' said at last Bulba, waking up from his revery. ' One would think you were a crowd of Tartars. Well, well, to the Evil One with your thoughts! Just take your pipes between your teeth, and let us have a smoke, and give our horses the spurs. Then we will fly that even a bird could not catch us ! '

" And the Cossaks, leaning over their horses, were lost in the grass. Now even their black caps could no longer be seen; only a track of trampled-down grass traced their swift flight.

" The sun had long been looking forth on the cleared heavens, and poured over the whole steppe its refreshing warmth-breathing light. Whatever was dim and sleepy in the Cossaks' souls suddenly fled; their hearts began to beat faster, like birds'.

" The farther they went, the more beautiful the steppe grew. In those days the vast expanse which now forms New Russia, to the very shores of the Black Sea, was green, virgin desert. The plough had never passed along the immeasurable waves of the wild plants. Horses alone, whom they hid, were trampling them down. Nothing in Nature could be more beautiful. The whole surface of the land presented a greenish-golden ocean, on which were sparkling millions of all manner of flowers. Through the thin high stalks of the grass were reaching forth the light-blue, dark-blue, and lilac-colored flowers ; the yellow broom-plant jumped out above, with its pyramid-like top. The white clover, with its parasol-shaped little caps, shone gayly on the surface. A halm of wheat, brought hither God knows whence, was playing the lonely dandy. By the thin roots of the grasses were gliding the prairie-chicks, stretching out their necks. The air was filled with a thousand different whistles of birds. In the sky floated immovably hawks, their wings spread wide, their eyes steadily fixed on the grass. The cry of a cloud of wild geese moving on the side was heard on a lake, Heaven knows how far off. With measured beating of its wings there rose from the grass a gull, and bathed luxuriously in the blue waves of the atmosphere. Now she is lost in the height, now she gleams as a dark point ; there, she has turned on her wings, and has sparkled in the sun! . . . The Devil take ye, ye steppes, how beautiful you are!"

8. If the height of the mount, swelling as it does the breast of the mountaineer, makes his spirit free by filling his lungs to their very roots, how much more must the steppe liberate the spirit of man by giving the eye an ever-fleeing circle to behold whithersoever it turn! How much more free than the mountaineer must the son of the steppe feel, for whom distance hath no terror, since go he never so far, he beholds the same sky, the same horizon, the same grass, and his cheek is fanned by the same breeze! To jump upon his faithful steed, to prick her sides with the spur, to be off in the twinkling of an eye with the swiftness of the wind, at the least discontent, is therefore as natural to the Russian of the South as it is for the Russian of the North to endure patiently in his place of birth whatever Fortune hath in store for him. The Cossak has therefore for ages been on' land what the sailor is on sea, — light-hearted, jolly when with comrades, melancholy when alone; but whether with his mates or alone, of a spirit

indomitably free. And Gogol was a Cossak. Southern Russia had not as yet produced a single great voice, because Southern Russia, New Russia, had as yet no aristocracy. Gogol is thus the only great Russian writer who sprang not from an autocracy whitewashed with Western culture, but from the genuine Russian people. It is this which makes Gogol the most characteristic of Russian writers.

9. Gogol was born in the province of Poltava, in 1810. His grandfather was an honored member of the government of the Cossak Republic, which at that time formed almost a state within the state. It was he that entertained his grandson with the stories of the life of the Cossaks, their adventures, their wars, as well as with the tales of devils, of apparitions, of which that country is full, and which form the principal amusement of the people during their long winter evenings.

10. We shall see later that the essential characteristic of Gogol's art was his wonderful power as a teller of a story. This came to him directly from the grandfather through the

father. But the father was already a man of a certain degree of culture. He was fond of reading, subscribed to the magazines, loved to entertain, and more than once had even private theatricals at his house.

11. The boy grew up at home till he was twelve years old. But at that age he was sent away to school at Nyezhin, with results questionable enough. The only signs of promise he showed were a strong memory and an honest but intense dislike of those studies which are only useful when forgotten. The problem as to the necessity of making children familiar with Timbuctoo, Popocatepetl, parallelopipeds, and relative dative and absolute ablative, the boy settled for himself in clearheaded boyish fashion. He hated mathematics, he hated the ancient languages. Accordingly, though he stayed three years under the professor of Latin, all he could learn was the first paragraph of a Latin Reader which begins with the instructive sentence: Universus mundus in duas distribuitur partes; from which circumstance poor Gogol was ever after known among his mates under

the name of Universus Mundus. Teachers and scholars therefore scorned poor Universus Mundus; but the boy faithfully kept a book under his desk during recitations, and read most diligently, leaving Universus Mundus to run its own course.

12. But if the boy did not lead his fellow-pupils in familiarity with Popocatepetl and parallelopiped, he did lead them in intellectual energy and practical life; a voracious reader, a passionate student of Zhukofsky and Pushkin, he founded not only a college review, which he filled mostly with his own contributions, but also a college theatre, which furnished entertainment not only to the boys themselves, but even to the citizens of the town. Nor did the boy rest until he saw his efforts towards founding a college library crowned with success.

13. This public spirit, which became in time all-absorbing to him, thus showed itself even in his boyhood. It was not long before the purpose of his life which hitherto manifested itself unconsciously now became the conscious part of his existence; and when in

1828 the boy left the Nyezhin Gymnasium, he was already filled with conscious desire to serve God with all his soul and man with all his heart. But as the body on its entrance into life must go through a baptism of water, so the soul on its entrance into life must go through a baptism of fire, and the fire to poor Gogol was scorching enough. Deeply religious towards God, nobly enthusiastic towards·men, the boy in his simplicity, innocence, and trustfulness found himself repelled by an unsympathetic and hampered by a misunderstanding world, which instead of encouraging the sympathy-hungry youth, was only too ready to laugh to scorn with its superior wisdom the dreams of the visionary. The home, the province, now becomes too narrow for the rapidly unfolding soul. To St. Petersburg he must go, the capital of talent, of aspiration, of hope, where are published the magazines so eagerly devoured in the days gone by, — to the capital, where dwell Zhukofsky and Pushkin. There his talents shall be recognized, and an appreciating world shall receive the new-comer with open arms. The arms of the world do indeed open on his arrival at St. Petersburg, but it is the cold embrace of want, of friend-lessness. In St. Petersburg begins for him a struggle for existence which well-nigh ruins him forever. Bread is not easily earned. Congenial society does not readily seek him out, and the sympathetic appreciation his starving soul craves is still as far as ever. Inevitable disappointment of hero-worship also quickly comes. When he calls at the door of the idolized Pushkin late in the morrow, he is told by the valet that the great man is deigning to be asleep at this late hour. " Ah, your master has been composing some heavenly song all night ! " " Not at all ; he has been playing cards till seven in the morning ! " And to complete his doom, his tender susceptible heart begins to flutter with right serious ado at the sight of a dame of high social position who hardly deigns to cast even a glance at the moneyless, ill-clad, clumsy, rustic lad, — sorrows enough for a soul far better equipped for battle with Fortune than this poor Cossak lad. Total ruin is now dangerously nigh. And here Gogol becomes high-handed. He must be off, away from this suffocation of disappointment and despair. He must seek new fields; if Fortune is not to be found in St. Petersburg, then it shall be sought beyond St. Petersburg; and if not in Russia, then out of Russia. Not him shall sportive Fortune flee; not him, the youth of merit, the youth of promise. In the days of yore he had charmed the good folk of Nye-zhin by his acting from the stage the part of an old woman. Wherefore not conquer Fortune as an old woman, if she favor not the young man? In a foreign land he might yet find his goal as an actor, and he decides to exile himself. Of moneys there are indeed none. Fortunately his mother, now already a widow, sends him some moneys wherewith to pay off their pledged estate. But the dutiful son keeps the moneys, advises his mother to take in return his share of his father's estate, and departs for the promised land. He goes to Germany, to Lubeck, to conquer Fortune as an actor.

14. Conquer Fortune he indeed did. For

in less than a month he found himself back in St. Petersburg, now a sober, a wiser man. The period of stress, of storm, was at an end, and henceforth letters were chosen as his life-long occupation. Bread, indeed, has to be earned by all manner of makeshifts, — now by serving as a scribe in some dreary government hall, now by reading off mechanically to university students what officially passes as lectures ; but the life of his soul, whatever his body might busy itself with, was henceforth given unto letters.

15. Henceforth, in order to make his life most fruitful unto men, which is his constant purpose, he is to write. But write what? Gogol gazes into his heart, and there finds the memories of the steppe, of the valiant Cossaks, their prowess and their freedom. His soul is filled at the sight of these with a tenderness and beauty which give him no rest until he pours them out over the pages of his book, and "Taras Bulba" is covered with a glory well-nigh unattained in any language since the days of Homer. For "Taras Bulba," though only one of several

stories in " Evenings on a Farm," is among
them what the star Sirius is in the already
glorious heavens of a November midnight.
As a thing of beauty, of simple grandeur, of
wild strength, of heroic nobility, as a song,
in short, I do not hesitate to affirm that it
finds its like only in the Iliad. It is an epic
song, and a song not of an individual soul
but of a whole nation.   Written down it
was indeed by the hands of Gogol, but com-
posed it was by the whole of Little Russia.
As the whole of heroic Greece sings in the
wrath of Achilles, so the whole of Cossak-
dom, which in its robust truth and manly
simplicity is not unlike heroic Greece, sings
in " Taras Bulba."

16. The poem is introduced as follows : —

" ' Just turn round, sonny ! Well, I declare
if you are not ridiculous ! What kind of a rig
have you on ? Why, you look like priests ! Are
they all dressed thus in the academy ? '

" With these words old Bulba met his two sons
who came home from the Kief seminary to their
father. His sons had just got down from their
horses. They were two sturdy fellows, still
looking out from under their brows just like

fresh seminary graduates. Their strong, healthy faces were covered with the first down, as yet untouched by a razor. They were much embarrassed at such reception by their father, and they stood motionless, with eyes fixed on the ground.

" ' Stand still, stand still; just let me get a good look at you,' he continued, as he turned them about. 'What long jackets you have on! What a jacket! Who ever heard of such jackets before! Just let one of you take a run, and see whether he would not tumble over, entangled in his coat-tails.'

" ' Don't laugh, father, don't laugh,' said at last the eldest.

" ' See how touchy he is! And why, pray, shall not I laugh?'

" ' Because! For even if you are my father, but if you laugh, by God, I will thrash you!'

" ' Well, well, well, did you ever! Is this the kind of a son you are? How? Your father?' said Taras Bulba, stepping back in surprise.

" ' Yes, even if you are my father. An insult I will stand from none.'

" ' How then do you wish to fight me? Boxing?'

" ' I don't care ; any way.'

" ' Well then, let us box,' said Bulba, rolling up his sleeves. 'I would like to see what sort of a boxer you are.'

" And father and son, instead of greeting

each other after the long separation, began to
give each other blows, now in the sides, now in
the ribs, now in the breast, now stepping back
and looking about, now coming forward again.

" ' Just see, good people, the old fool has become crazy,' said the pale, thin, good mother,
who was standing on the threshold and had not
been able to embrace her darling boys. ' The
children come home after an absence of over a
year, and he gets it into his head, God knows
what, to box with them.'

" ' Yes, he fights finely,' said Bulba, stopping.
' Good, by God ! ' he continued, catching a little
breath. ' So, yes, he will make a fine Cossak,
even without preliminary trial. ' Well, welcome, sonny ; come kiss me.' And father and
son began to kiss each other. ' Good, my son.
Thrash everybody as you have given it to me.
Don't let him go ! But I must insist, yours is
a ridiculous rig. What rope is this, dangling
down there ! ' "

17. Bulba is so pleased with his boys that
he decides to take them the very next day to
the syetch, the republic of the Cossaks, and
there initiate them in the wild, glorious service. The mother's grief at the unexpected
loss of her boys, as well as the parting itself,
is thus described by Gogol : —

" Night had just enclosed the sky in its embrace ; but Bulba always retired early.   He
spread himself out on the mat and covered himself with the sheep-skin ; for the night air was
quite fresh, and Bulba, moreover, was fonder
of warmth when at home.   He soon began to
snore, and it was not long before the entire
household did the like.   Whatever lay in the
various corners of the court began to snore
and to whiz.   Before everybody else fell asleep
the watchman ; for in honor of the return of the
young Cossaks he had drunk more than the
rest.

"The poor mother alone was awake.   She
nestled herself close to the heads of her dear
boys, who were lying side by side.   She combed
their young, carelessly bunched-up locks, and
moistened them with her tears.   She gazed
upon them with all her eyes, with all her feelings ; she was transformed into nothing but
sight, and yet she could not look enough at
them.   She had fed them from her own breast.
She had raised them, had fondled them, and
now she sees them again only for a moment !
' My boys, my darling boys, what is to become
of ye, what is in store for ye ? ' she spake, and
the tears halted on her wrinkles, which had
changed her once handsome face.   In truth,
she was to be pitied, as every woman of that
rough age was to be pitied.   Only a moment had

she lived in love, only in the first fever of passion, in the first fever of youth, and already her
rough charmer had forsaken her for the sword,
for his companions, for the wild excitement of
war. During the year she saw her husband
perhaps two — three times, and then again for
some years there was not even a trace of him.
And when they did come together, when they
did live together, what sort of life was hers!
She suffered insult, even blows. She received
her fondlings as a kind of alms; she felt herself
a strange creature in this assemblage of wifeless
knights, to whom the loose life of the Cossaks
had given a coloring sombre enough. Youth
flashed by her joylessly, and her beautiful fresh
cheeks and fingers had withered away without kisses, and were covered with premature
wrinkles. All her love, all her tenderness,
whatever was soft and passionate in woman,
was merged in her into the one feeling of a
mother. With heat, with passion, with tears,
like a gull of the steppe, she was cir ᴏ
her babes. Her boys, her darling boys, are to
be taken from her, — taken from her never to be
seen again. Who knows, perhaps at the very
first battle the Tartar shall cut off their heads,
and she shall not know where their castaway
bodies are lying to be pecked in pieces by the
bird of prey, while for every drop of their blood
she would have given up her whole life. Groan-

ing, she looked into their eyes, when almighty
sleep began to close them, and she thought to
herself, 'Perhaps Bulba will change his mind
when he wakes, and put off the departure for a
day or two; perhaps he has decided to go off so
soon because he had taken a little too much.'

"The moon had for some time been shining
from the high heavens upon the whole court,
its sleeping folk, the thick clump of willows and
the high wild oats in which was drowned the
fence surrounding the court. Still she was sitting at the head-side of her darling boys, not
taking her eyes off them for a moment, and not
even thinking of sleep. The horses, already
feeling the morrow, had all lain down in the
grass, and ceased feeding. The upper leaves
of the willows began to whisper, and little by
little a whispering wave descended along them
to the very bottom. But she was still sitting
up till daybreak, not at all tired, but inwardly
wishing that the night might last only longer.
From the steppe came up the loud neighing of
a colt; red bars gleamed brightly along the
sky. . . .

"When the mother saw that at last her sons
also were now seated on their horses, she rushed
to the youngest, in whose features there seemed
to be more of a certain tenderness, seized his
spur, clung to his saddle, and with despair in her
eyes, she held fast to him. Two robust Cos-

saks took gently hold of her and carried her
into the house. But when they rode out beyond the gates, with the lightness of a wild
stag, incompatible with her years, she ran out
beyond the gates, and with incomprehensible
strength she stopped the horse and embraced
one of her sons with a kind of crazy, feelingless
feverishness. Again she was carried off.

"The young Cossaks rode in silence, and held
back their tears in fear of their father, who,
however, was for his part not wholly at ease,
though he tried not to betray himself. The sky
was gray; the green was sparkling with a glare;
the birds were singing as if in discord. The
Cossaks, after riding some distance, looked back.
Their farm-house seemed to have gone down
into the ground. Above ground were seen only
the two chimneys of their modest house, and
the tops of the trees, along whose branches
they had been leaping like squirrels [in their
childhood.] There still was stretched before
them that prairie which held for them the
whole history of their life, from the years
when they made somersaults on its thick grass,
to the years when they would await there the
black-browed Cossak dame as she was tripping
swiftly along with her fresh light step. Now
they see only the pole over the well, and the
cart-wheel, tied to its top, alone sticks out on
the sky. And now the plain they had just passed

seems a distant mount, hiding everything behind it. . . . Farewell, childhood, and play, and
all, and all ! . . . "

18. I had hoped at first to be able to give
you a few passages from this noblest of epic
poems which might·give you some idea of
its wild, thrilling beauty : the jolly life at the
syetch ; the sudden transformation of the
frolicking, dancing, gambling crowd into a
well-disciplined army of fierce warriors, which
strikes terrors into the hearts of the Poles.
I hoped to be able to give you Gogol's own
account of the slaying of Andrei, his youngest son, by Bulba himself, because, bewitched
by a pair of fair eyes, he became traitor to
the Cossaks.   I wished to quote to you the
stoic death, under the very eyes of his father,
of Ostap, the oldest son, torn as he is alive to
pieces, not a sound escaping his lips, but at
the very last moment, disheartened at the sea
of hostile faces about him, crying only, "Father, seest thou all this?"   I wished to quote
to you Bulba's own terrible death, nailed
alive to a tree, which is set on fire under him ;
the old hero, still intent on the salvation of

his little band, while the smoke envelops him, cries, as he beholds the movement of the enemy, " To the shore, comrades, to the shore ! Take the path to the left ! "   But I found I should have to quote to you the entire book ; for there is not a single page of this poem from which beauty does not shine forth with dazzling radiance.   Homer often nods in the Iliad, but in " Taras Bulba " Gogol never nods.   And as the painter of old on being asked to remove the curtain that the picture might be seen replied, " The curtain *is* the picture," so can I only say to you, " Read ' Taras Bulba,' and it shall be its own commentary unto you ! "

19. With " Taras Bulba," Gogol had reached the height as a singer.   On this road there was no longer any progress for his soul, and to remain a cheerful, right-glad singer in the midst of the sorrowing, overburdened country was impossible to a man of Gogol's earnestness.   For his first and last end was to serve his country.   'T is well, if he could serve it by letters, equally well, if he could serve it by his simple life.   Gogol,

therefore, now decided to devote the rest of his days to the unveiling of the ills to which the Russian Colossus was subject, in the hope that the sight of the ugly cancer would help its removal. Thus he became the conscious protester, the critic of autocracy; and he became such because his gifts were best fitted for such labor. For coupled with his unsurpassed gift of story-telling was another distinct trait of the Cossak in him, — the ability of seeing good-humoredly the frailties of man; and his humor, undefiled by the scorn of the cynic, proved a most powerful weapon in his hands. Ridicule has ever proved a terror to corruption. But in the hands of Gogol this ridicule became a weapon all the more powerful because it took the shape of impersonal humor where the indignation of the author was kept out of sight, so that even stern Nicolas himself, the indirect source of the very corruption satirized in " The Revisor," could laugh, while a listener to the play, until the tears ran down his cheeks and his sides ached. The corruption of provincial officials, which is the natural sore following all autocratic blood-poisoning, found merciless treatment at the hands of Gogol in his comedy " The Revisor." Its plot is briefly as follows : —

20. The mayor of a small city receives suddenly the news that a revisor, a secret examiner, is on the way from the capital to investigate his administration. Quickly he assembles all the worthies of the town, the director of schools, of prisons, of hospitals, all of whom have but too guilty consciences, and they all decide on measures of escape from his wrath. They march in file to the hotel where the supposed Revisor lodges. There for some days had been dwelling a young penniless good-for-nothing whom the officials mistake for the dreaded Revisor. The young man is surprised, but soon accepts the situation, and plays his part admirably. Presents and bribes are sent him from all sides ; he borrows money right and left, makes love to the mayor's wife as well as to his daughter, and finally engages to marry the — daughter. The mayor is happy and honored as never before, and relying

upon the protection of the Revisor outrages the community now more than ever. At last the pseudo-revisor departs with all the gifts and loans, and in a few days the real Revisor actually arrives, to the astonishment and dismay of the officials, who till now had felt secure in their misdeeds.

21. "The Revisor" is indeed a great comedy, the equal of Griboyedof's "Misfortune from Brains." As a comedy it is therefore the inferior of none, — neither of Terence, nor of Molière. But as a work of art it cannot rank as high as "Taras Bulba," because no comedy can ever be as great a thing of beauty as an epic poem. What rouses laughter cannot rank as high as what rouses tender emotion. Moreover, with the passing away of the generation familiar with the corruption it satirizes, the comedy often becomes unintelligible save to scholars. Hence the utter valuelessness to us of to-day of the comedies of Aristophanes as works of wit. Their only value to-day is as fragmentary records of Greek manners. The comedy is thus writ not for all times, but only for *a* time; while

"Taras Bulba," though generations come
and generations go, will ever appeal unto
men as a thing of imperishable beauty. But
while "The Revisor" is below "Taras Bulba"
as a work of art, it is far above it as a work
of purpose, and has accordingly accomplished
a greater result. For "Taras Bulba" can
only give pleasure, though it be read for
thousands of years after "The Revisor" has
been forgotten. It will indeed give a noble
pleasure, at which the soul need not blush,
still it is only a pleasure. But "The Revisor" has helped to abolish corruption, has
fought the Evil One, has therefore done
work which, transient though it be, *must* be
done to bring about the one result which
alone is permanent, — the kingdom of heaven
upon earth ; the kingdom of truth, the kingdom of love, the kingdom of worship. And
whatever helps towards the establishment of
that on earth must be of a higher rank than
what only gives pleasure unto the soul.

22. The success of "The Revisor" spurred
the young Gogol on to further effort, and he
now resolved to give utterance to protest

against another crying wrong of Russian life, which in its consequences was far more disastrous to the country than official corruption. Gogol now undertook to lay bare the ills of serfdom. His soul had long since been searching for its activity a field as wide as life itself. With Gogol, as with all lofty souls before they find their truest self, aspiration ever soared above execution. Now, however, the time had arrived when his gifts could execute whatever his soul conceived; and his mighty spirit at last found fitting expression in " Dead Souls." Accordingly " Dead Souls " is not so much a story, a story of an event or of a passion, as a panorama of the whole country. In his search for Dead Souls, Tchichikof has to travel through the length and breadth of the land; through village and through town, through sunshine and through storm, by day and by night, through the paved imperial post-road as well as through the forsaken cross-lane. This enables Gogol to place before the reader not only the governor of the province, the judge, and the rich landowner, the possessor of hundreds of souls, but also the poverty-stricken, well-nigh ruined landowner; not only the splendor of the city, but also the squalor of the hamlet; not only the luxury of an invited guest, but also the niggardliness of the hotel-boarder. "Dead Souls" is thus a painting in literature, — what Kaulbach's "Era of the Reformation" is in history. And the originality of the execution lies in the arrangement which presents Russia in a view unseen as yet even by Pushkin, who knew his country but too well. Gogol may be said to have discovered Russia for the Russian, as Haxthausen discovered it for the West, and as De Tocqueville discovered America for the Americans. "Great God!" exclaimed Pushkin, on reading "Dead Souls," "I had no idea Russia was such a dark country!" And this is the characteristic of this among the greatest of paintings of Russian life, — the faithful gloom which overhangs the horizon. In spite of its humor, the impression left on the mind by "Dead Souls" is that of the sky during an equinoctial storm; and on closing the book, in spite of your laughter, you feel as if you had just returned from a funeral. The

work is conceived in humor, designed to
rouse laughter, but it is laughter which shines
through tears. It is the laughter of a soul
which can no longer weep outwardly, but
inwardly. It is the same laughter which Lessing indulged in when his wife and child were
snatched from him both at once. For six
long weary years he had battled with poverty,
disappointment, and despair, to reach at last
in joy the goal of his life ; he weds at last
his beloved dame, and lo, the close of the
first year of his paradise finds mother and
babe lying side by side — lifeless. Lessing
laughs. He writes to a friend : "The poor
little fellow hath early discovered the sorrows
of this earth, so he quickly hied himself hence,
and lest he be lonely, took his mother along."
There is laughter here, indeed, but the soul
here laughs with a bleeding, torn, agonized
heart. It is the same laughter which was
roused among the disciples of Christ when
they heard their Master utter the grim joke,
"Verily, it is easier for a camel to go through
the eye of the needle, than for a rich man to
enter the kingdom of heaven." Such laughter
is Gogol's in "Dead Souls." Gogol had now

learned to comprehend the words of his
friend Ivanof, — " Christ never laughed."

23. I dwell on this phase of Gogol's laughter, because Gogol in his " Dead Souls " unconsciously recognized that behind everything
laughable there is at bottom not a comedy
but a tragedy; that at bottom it is the cold
head only which laughs, and not the warm
heart. Think, and thou shalt laugh; feel,
and thou shalt weep. Judgment laughs, sympathy weeps. Sin, wickedness, O my friends,
is not a thing to laugh at, but a thing to weep
at; and your English humorists have not yet
learned, when they must laugh at vice and
sin, to laugh at it with a heart full of woe.
Swift is steeped in vinegar; Fielding's humor is oiled and sugar-coated; Dickens can
never laugh unless with convulsive explosion;
Thackeray sneers, and George Eliot is almost
malicious with her humor; and the only man
in English literature who is sick at heart while
he laughs is not even counted among the humorists, — Carlyle. In English literature the
laughter of Cervantes in Don Quixote is unknown; but the humor of Cervantes is nearest that of Gogol. Gogol's laughter is the

laughter of a man who so loves his fellow-men that their weakness is his pain; and the warmest corner in all Russia for the very men Gogol satirizes would doubtless have been found in his own heart. It is this spirit in which " Dead Souls " is writ which makes " Dead Souls " a model for all humorous writing.

24. I can give you, however, no nobler example of this laughter through tears by Gogol than the following closing passage from his " Memoirs of a Maniac." You remember that during his stay at St. Petersburg, Gogol fell in love with a woman far above his social rank. In this piece of only twenty pages Gogol paints the mental condition of an humble office-scribe, who, falling in hopeless love with the daughter of his chief, loses his poor mind. After various adventures he at last imagines himself King Ferdinand of Spain, is locked up in an asylum, and is beaten whenever he speaks of himself as the king. And this is the last entry in the poor maniac's diary : —

" No, I no longer can endure it. God, what are they doing to me ! They pour cold water on my head! They neither mind me, nor do they see me, nor do they hear me. What have I done to them? What do they wish of poor me? What can I give them? I have nothing. I have no more strength. I no longer can endure all their torment; my head is afire, and all around me is in a whirl. Save me! Take me! Give me a span of horses swift as the wind! Get up, driver; ring, little bell; off ye horses, and carry me off from this world! Away, away, that I see nothing more, —nothing. Ha! there is the sky vaulting before me; a star sparkles in the distance; there rushes the forest with its dark trees, and the moon. A gray fog spreads under my feet; a string resounds in the fog; on one side is the sea, on the other Italy; now Russian huts are already in sight. Is this my home which rises blue in the distance? Is it my mother sitting at the window? Dear mother, save your poor boy; drop a tearlet on his sick head. See how they torment him; press your poor orphan to your breast! There is no place for him on this wide earth! He is chased! Dear mother, have pity on your sick babe! . . . By the way, do you know, the Emperor of Algeria has a wart under his very nose!"

25. With the completion of the first part of " Dead Souls," Gogol had reached the height

as a protester. He had now exhausted this side of his life, — the side which was the essence of his being, the side which made him the individual person as distinct from the rest of men. After the first part of " Dead Souls " his message unto men was a thing of the past. Henceforth, whatever he could do, could only be a repetition of his former burning words, and hence only a weaker utterance. This is precisely what happens to most men of letters when they persist in speech after naught is left them to say. You need only be reminded of Bryant in this country, who had exhausted all the music of his soul in his younger days, and of Tennyson in England, who as shadowy Lord Tennyson can only ignobly borrow of marrowy Alfred Tennyson. But Gogol was too conscientious an artist to allow himself to become prey of such literary sin. If produce he must, it shall be no repetition of his former self, but in a still higher field than mere protest. Accordingly, he attempted in his second part of " Dead Souls " to paint an ideal Russia, just as in the first part he had painted the real Russia. Here, however, he undertook what was above his genius: the skylark is indeed a noble bird, but is unfit for the flight of the eagle. Who was by nature only a protester could not by sheer force of will be transformed into the idealizing constructor. And of this, Gogol himself soon became aware. To the very end he was discontented with his second part, and finally, before his death, gave it over to the flames.

26. The heavenly spark which gleamed within him could not, however, be put out. Letters proper he at last indeed forsook, but he now became profoundly religious; he gave up all his possessions to the poor, and when he needed moneys wherewith to make a pilgrimage to what was to him a veritably Holy Land, he had to publish some of his intimate correspondence.

27. This work proved the bitterness of the rest of his days. It roused a clamor against the poor author altogether out of proportion to the slight merit of the work. Gogol was denounced on all sides as a renegade; the relentless accuser of autocracy in "The Re-

visor " could not be forgiven for the spirit of
Christian humility and resignation to the will
of God which breathed from these letters. It
was in the forties. Those were the days when
a Hegelian wave went over Russian minds.
God had been philosophized away to make
place for the Absolute, and even school-boys
came home to announce the astounding news
that there was no longer any God. Who was
not a doubter, a disbeliever, was unhesitat-
ingly declared an imbecile ; and Gogol's correspondence, breathing as it does the spirit of
the deepest godfulness, came upon his friends
like a note of discord at a concert. His
friends declared him insane, and all manner
of advice offered, which could not fail to
make him truly insane. The already melancholy Gogol now became lonely, dejected,
and sought consolation now more than ever
in fasting and prayer. Poor Gogol had not
yet learned that complete salvation is found
not in praying, but in doing. While his ills
therefore increased his devotion, his devotion
likewise in turn increased his ills ; his body
became emaciated, his mind was wrecked,

and early in 1852 he was found one morning
starved to death, prostrated before the holy
images, in front of which he had spent his
last days.

28. Next to Tolstoy, Gogol is perhaps the
most lovable figure in Russian literature. I
say lovable, because he was at bottom a hapless man, — a man who had fed on his own
mighty heart.   There is a Carlylesqueness
about his woe that makes his life immeasurably pitiful. Pushkin's sorrow one finds it
difficult to lament deeply, since it was mostly
of his own making ; but Gogol's was the sorrowful lot of all heaven-aspiring souls who
have not yet attained the last, safest haven
of rest in God, — that haven from which the
soul no longer cries in agony of spirit, " My
God, my God, why hast thou forsaken me ! "
but rather, " Father, thou knowest wherefore
all this is ; thy will be done ! "   His soul in
its loneliness and restlessness knew nor sympathy nor appreciation of what was to him
his deepest life ; and this the loving soul
ever craves most hungeringly.   When the
great soul had departed, gone irrevocably,

8

men readily enough recognized that the light
of Israel had gone out; but the recognition
came too late, the love came when it could
no longer heal his wounded spirit.

29. My friends, " Taras Bulba " will thrill
your soul with inexpressible beauty. Gogol's
" Revisor " will amuse you. His " Dead
Souls " will instruct you ; but his life, if you
study it faithfully, should prove his greatest
work unto you, for it should stir you, — stir
you to tenderness, stir you to sympathy, stir
you to compassion for those sufferers, the like
of Gogol, who are never wanting, in whatever age, in whatever clime, in whatever
walk of life. Would to God, my friends, you
could carry away from Gogol's life with you
this lesson : In your very midst, perhaps this
very day, there doubtless walks among you
some mighty spirit, some hungry soul. Seek
him out, find him out, that not of ye at least
shall be said those immeasurably sorrowful
words which could be said of the countless
friends of Gogol, — they came with their
sympathy — too late !

LECTURE IV.

———◆———

TURGENEF.

1. IN the history of Russian letters, Ivan Turgenef is the most complex figure. Nay, with the exception of Shakespeare he is perhaps the most complex figure in all literature. He is universal, he is provincial; he is pathetic, he is sneering; he is tender, he is merciless; he is sentimental, he is frigid. He can be as compact as Tacitus, and as prolix as Thackeray. He can be as sentimental as Werther, and as heartless as Napoleon. He can cry with the bird, grow with the grass, and hum with the bee; he can float with the spirits, and dream with the fevered. He is everywhere at home: in the novel, in the story, in the sketch, in the diary, in the epistle. Whatever form of composition he

touches, let once his genius be mature, and it turns to gold under his hands. On reading through his ten volumes you leave him with the feeling that you have just emerged from the virgin forests of South America; your head is full of monkeys frolicking about, with an occasional cocoanut shot at you; your head is full of the birds with their variegated plumage, of the fragrance of the flowers, of the dusk about you, and of the primeval still-ness of the forest. And the collective impres-sion of the writer, the man, left upon you is that of some invisible but consummate artist who had been passing before you all manner of photographs made lurid by the glare of the stereopticon: photograph now of sunset cloud, now of lover's scene in the lane, now of a dyspeptic, long-haired, wrinkled old man. The writer Turgenef has thus been for years an enigma. Katkof, the pillar of Russian au-tocracy, claims him as his, and the revolu-tionists claim him as theirs; the realists point to him as one of the apostles of their new gospel, and the idealists point to him as the apostle of theirs. Now he defies public opin-

ion by befriending an obnoxious exile, now
he shrinks before it by disclaiming almost his
acquaintance. Between the contending parties, poor Turgenef shared the fate of the
child of the women who did *not* come to
King Solomon for advice in their dispute
about its mother. The poor child was pulled
by each until disfigured for life. So Turgenef
between the different parties, each claiming
him as its own, remained homeless, almost
friendless, to the end of his days, belonging
to none ; and though surrounded by all manner of society and companionship which fame,
wealth, and position could give, he was yet at
bottom solitary, for he went through the world
a man who was misunderstood.

2. His position in letters is therefore anom-
alous. Russians blame him, but read him ;
and Americans praise him, and read him not.
Englishmen quote him, Frenchmen write essays on him, and Germans write books about
him ; but all agree in wondering at him, all
agree in not comprehending him. And yet
Turgenef's life and the purpose of his books
is plain enough to him that comes to view

him with eyes as yet uncovered by partisan glasses. Turgenef the realist, Turgenef the idealist, is enigmatic enough ; but once understood that Turgenef was the literary warrior against what was to him a mortal enemy, and his whole life and all his important works at once become explicable, consistent.

3. For man is something more than the mere sum of his abilities. Behind all the forces of the man, whether of body or of mind, there stands the soul, which uses them for purposes of its own, be they for better or for worse. And of these there is always one which in time becomes the absorbent of all its life, the essence of all its being ; and such purpose is soon found in the life of every man who lives, and not merely exists ; such purpose is soon found in the mightiest as well as in the frailest, in the loftiest as well as in the lowest. And till such purpose is understood, the life of the man is to beholders what the flower is to the eye when looked at through a microscope,— an expanse of mere tissue, rough, formless, confusing ; but such purpose once understood, the soul is trans-

formed to the beholder as if made of glass,
transparent, uniform, simple.

4. Such purpose runs like a woof through
the whole being of Turgenef. He is a hunt-
er, he is a clubman, he is a philanthropist, he
is an artist; but he is first of all a warrior,
because he is first of all a lover of his country, and a hater of what oppresses it. He
does indeed much else besides fighting for
the emancipation of the land of his birth;
but he does it in the same spirit in which sensible folk go to dinners not for the sake of
eating, to receptions not for the sake of being
received, and wear kid gloves in summer not
for the sake of keeping the hands warm;
these things, meaningless in themselves, are
only incidentals in the life of the spirit, which
alone can be said to have any meaning.

5. Turgenef, then, is the fighter. This accounts for what is otherwise a strange phenomenon in Turgenef's art. In his " Memoirs
of a Sportsman," in which he first aimed his
blows consciously against serfdom, his muse
busies itself not with life normal, but with
life abnormal; not with every-day characters,

but with such as are seen rarely ; not with fre-
quented places, but with unfrequented places.
The " Memoirs of a Sportsman " is a collection of sketches which form a sort of variety
museum of all manner of bizarre and even
grotesque figures. Critics naturally marvelled
at this ; and as in the days of old, men explained the effects of morphine by saying
that it contained the soporific principle, and
the action of the pump by nature's abhorring
a vacuum, so critics explained this fact, so
strange in the healthy, clear-eyed, measure-
loving Turgenef, by saying that he had a natural fondness for the fantastic and the strange.
In truth, however, the choice of his subjects
was part of his very art as a warrior. He
wished to strike, to rouse ; and here the ex-
traordinary is ever more effective than the ordinary. It was the same design which made
the otherwise generous, tender Wendell Phillips adopt a personal mode of warfare in his
struggle against slavery with a bitterness almost Mephistophelian. And the same purpose made Turgenef, against the dictates of
his muse, choose strange characters for his

sketches. Both Phillips and Turgenef here
sacrificed their feelings to their cause : the
one sacrificed to his purpose even his love
for his fellow-men; the other, even his love
for his art.

6. One other strange fact in the art of Turgenef is explained by this fighting essence of
his being. There is no growth, development,
visible in Turgenef. He lived to what is for
Russian men of letters an advanced age : he
died when over sixty years old ; yet, beginning
with his first great work of art, " Rudin," and
ending with his last great work of art, " Virgin Soil," through all his masterpieces, he
remains the same. His six great novels,
" Rudin," " A Nest of Noblemen," " On the
Eve," " Fathers and Sons," " Smoke," and
" Virgin Soil," form indeed an ascending
scale, but not as works of art ; as such, they
are all on the same highest plane. And it
would be difficult to find any canon of art
according to which one could be placed
above the other. Only when viewed as different modes of warfare, do they represent
the different stages of his soul's life ; but this

only in so far as they reflect at the same time the state of the enemy's forces, against whom he found it necessary to re-equip himself from time to time. As an artist, then, Turgenef is not progressive; when his art comes to him, it comes like Minerva from Jupiter's head, — fully made, fully armed; and had it even come undeveloped, it would have had, in his case, to remain thus. For growth, development, needs time, needs leisure, needs reflection, needs rest; and of all this, on the field of battle, there is none to be had. Onward or backward, conquer or perish, but stand still on the field of battle thou must not. And while it was not given to Turgenef to conquer, neither was it given to the enemy to conquer him. Turgenef, therefore, as he lived a fighter, so he died a fighter.

7. Turgenef, then, had a life-long enemy; this enemy was Russian autocracy.

8. Born in 1818, in the same year with the autocrat of Russia, who afterwards dreaded him as his *bête noir*, he already in his childhood had the opportunity to learn the weight of the iron hand of Nicolas. Scarcely was

he seven years old when the news came to
his father's household that the family name
so dear to them, and hitherto a synonym of
honor both in and out of Russia, had been dis-
graced; that Nicolai Turgenef, one of the
most faithful servants of the country under
Alexander I., the younger of the two celebrated brothers, and a near relative of Ivan,
had been sentenced to Siberian hard labor for
life, — sentenced under circumstances which
could not but shock the sense of justice not
only of the trustful boy, but also of those
whom maturer age had accustomed to the
methods of the government. Nicolai Turgenef was condemned as one of the Decembrists, and the days of the youth of Ivan were
the days when the Decembrists were looked
up to as the first martyrs of Russian liberty.
Pushkin, the friend of the leaders of the in-
surrection, and the singer of the " Ode to Liberty," was then worshipped by the youth of
Russia as poet was worshipped never before;
to be related to the Decembrists was therefore a privilege, and to oppose autocracy in
thought at least thus became a kind of family

pride. Moreover, contrary to most Russian aristocrats, Sergei Turgenef conducted the early education of his gifted son himself; and the son of the conscientious father, when taken out into the world, could not but feel the discord between the peaceful life, rigid conduct, and high ideals of his home on the one hand, and the gloomy struggle for existence, lax morals of the officials, and the low standards of the world about him on the other. When Turgenef therefore was introduced into society, he was already saturated with revolutionary ideas, and it was not long before he found the atmosphere of his native land stifling; and already, at the age of nineteen, he had to face the question whether to stay and endure, or — to flee. The boy of nineteen cannot endure; go then from Russia he must, but go — whither? Fortunately, just beyond the western border there lay a country which had already proved the promised land of others equally defiant with Turgenef. Germany already harbored Stankevitch, Granofsky, Katkof, and Bakunin. The youth of Russia of those days had metaphorically cried to the Germans what a thousand years before them the Slavs had cried literally to the Varangians : " Our land is wide, and overflowing with abundance ; but of order in it there is none. Come ye, therefore, and rule over us, and restore order among us ! " Germany thus became the land of milk and honey for the Russians hungry in spirit. Whatever had any ambition looked to a visit to Germany with the same longing with which a Mohammedan looks to the shrines of Mecca.

9. Berlin was the first halting-station of the pilgrims ; Böck was lecturing there on Greek literature, Zumpt on Roman antiquities, and Werder was expounding the philosophy of the man who boasted or complained of being understood by only one man, and that one misunderstood him. To these masters in the education of hair-splitting flocked almost all who became celebrated afterwards in Russia's public life, and even the government was sending students to Berlin at public expense. To these masters Turgenef also went, hearing Greek literature and Roman an-

tiquities by day, and committing to memory
the elements of Greek and Latin grammar
by night. For in the Russian university,
where Turgenef had hitherto spent two years,
the professors were appointed not because of
their knowledge of Latin and Greek, but because of their knowledge of military tactics.

10. When after two years Turgenef returned to his native land, he brought back
with him, indeed, a high knowledge of Latin
grammar, but a total ignorance of the highest
aims of life. He brought back with him a
religious scepticism, and a metaphysical pessimism, which colored henceforth his whole
life, and therefore his artistic works. For
those were the days when men yet believed
that the great problems of the soul in its relation to the gods and to men could be solved
not so much by living and by doing, as by
disputing and by talking; those were the
days when the philosopher's stone, turning all
things into gold, was sought not in a rule for
the conduct of life, such as "Love thy neighbor," or "Do unto others," but rather in the
barren, egg-dancing, acrobatically-balanced

formula, "What is, is right." Those were the days when Hegel was supreme in philosophy because of his obscurity, as Browning is now supreme in poetry because of his; the shrivelled, evaporated, dead grain of wheat was prized all the more because it had been searched out with painful toil from the heap of chaff. "By their fruits ye shall know them." The fruit of the deep study of Browning is an intimate knowledge of the use of English particles; and the fruit of the devoted study of Hegel was an intimate knowledge of metaphysical verbiage: being, substance, essence, and absolute. But of life-giving nourishment there was none to be had. The barrenness of all this, Turgenef indeed soon did perceive, but when the disenchantment came, his blood was already poisoned; his very being was eaten into by doubt, and almost to the very end of his days Turgenef remained a fatalistic sceptic, a godless pessimist; not till his old age did he espy the promised land. It was only when he witnessed with his own eyes the boundless self-sacrifice of the revolutionists, when the old man was moved by the heroism of the young Sophie Bardine even to the kissing of the very sheet upon which the girl's burning words to her judges were printed, — then, indeed, he regained his faith. He now hoped for his country, and stood even ready to become the head of the revolutionary movement in Russia; but for his artistic career all this came too late. In fact, his faith in God he never regained, though his hope for man did come back at last in his old age with the glow of his younger days.

11. This fundamental philosophic scepticism which had poisoned Turgenef's mind throughout the best years of his life accounts for a striking change which in time took place in the method of his art. Hitherto his art had been photographic of individuals. His "Memoirs of a Sportsman" is a gallery, not of ideals, not of types, but of actual men, — a gallery put on exhibition for the same end for which the rogues' gallery is exposed at the police headquarters. It is a means towards the welfare of the country. But after that book, when the scepticism had become part

of his being, his method changes. For he
now becomes convinced that the misrule of
Russia is not so much due to the government
as to the people themselves; that existence
is in itself evil; that salvation, therefore, if it
can come at all, must come not from without,
but from within; that reform, therefore, was
needed not so much for the institution, as for
the men themselves. And to him men are
diseased. He no longer therefore paints individual men, but henceforth he paints types;
just as the physician first studies the disease
not as affecting this patient or that, but as
likely to affect all men, every man.

12. For much of this scepticism before life
and irreverence before God Turgenef had to
thank the paternal government of his father-
land. There are indeed those to whom sorrow comes like a messenger from the skies
above, and lifts them heavenward on its wings.
Turgenef alas! was not one of these. His
was one of those souls whom sorrow deprives
not only of the joys of the present, but also
of the hopes of the future; and the government saw to it that of sorrows poor Turge-

nef have enough. Homelessness is an afflic-
tion to all sons of Adam, but to none is the
sorrow of exile so intense as to the Russian.
And to exile Turgenef was soon driven.
Hid under glowing pictures of nature and
fascinating figures of men, the real meaning
of the "Memoirs of a Sportsman," while
they appeared in detached sketches, eluded
readily enough the Argus-eyed censor. But
when these sketches were gathered into a living book, then whatever had eye could behold,
and whatever had ear could hear, their heavenly message. The book therefore creates
a sensation, the censor is astir, hurried con-
sultation takes place, his Majesty himself
is roused; but all this too late; the living
book can no longer be strangled. The government saw that the monster was hydra-headed,
and resolved to let it alone rather than by
cutting one of its heads to rouse twenty in its
stead. The book then was spared, but the
writer was henceforth doomed; and the occasion for the final blow is soon enough at
hand. The great Gogol had at last departed.
The enthusiastic Turgenef writes a letter about

the dead master, and calls him a great man.
" In my land only he is great with whom I
speak, and only while I am speaking with
him," had said Paul the father ; and Nicolas
proved a worthy son. " In Russia there shall
be no great men," saith the Tsar ; and Turgenef is arrested. High-stationed dame indeed
intercedes for the gifted culprit. " But remember, madame," she is told, " he called
Gogol a great man." " Ah," high-stationed
protectress replies, " I knew not that he com-
mitted *that* crime ! " Which crime, accordingly, Turgenef expiates with one month's
imprisonment in the dungeon, and two years'
banishment to his estates. Only when the
heir to the throne himself appeased his en-
raged sire was Turgenef allowed to go in
peace. Once master over himself again, Turgenef hesitated no longer. He loved, indeed,
his country much, but he loved freedom more ;
and like a bird fresh from the cage away flew
Turgenef beyond the sea. The migrating bird
returns, indeed, in the spring ; but for Turgenef
there was no longer any spring on Russian soil,
and once abroad, he became an exile for life.

13. I have said that the heroes of his six great novels are not photographs, but types. I venture to say that neither Turgenef himself nor any other Russian ever knew *a* Bazarof, *a* Paul Kirsanof, *a* Rudin, *a* Nezhdanof. But as in the generic image of Francis Galton the traits of all the individuals are found whose faces entered into the production of the image, so in the traits of Turgenef's types every one can recognize some one of *his* acquaintance. And such is the life which the master breathes into his creations, that they become not only possible to the reader, but they actually gain flesh and blood in his very presence.

14. And of these types, Turgenef, in harmony with the advance of his own warfare, has furnished a progressive series. Accordingly the earliest depicted under the impression of profound despair is the type of the superfluous man, — the man, who not only *does* nothing, but *can* do nothing, struggle he never so hard. And the superfluous man not only *is* impotent, but he *knows* his impotence, so that he is dead in soul as well as in body.

This brief sketch of a living corpse, written as early as 1850, forms thus the prologue, as it were, to all his future tragedies. From this depth of nothingness Turgenef, however, soon rises to at least the semblance of strength; and while Rudin is at bottom as impotent as Tchulkaturin, he at least pretends to strength. Rudin, then, is the hero of phrases, the boaster; he promises marvels, he charms, he captivates; but it all ends in words, and Rudin perishes as needlessly as he lived needlessly. In "Fathers and Sons," however, Bazarof is no longer a talker; he already rises to indignation and rebellion; he *lives out* his spirit, and stubbornly resists society, religion, institutions. From Bazarof Turgenef ascends still higher to Nezhdanof in "Virgin Soil," whose aggressive attitude is already unmistakable. Nezhdanof no longer indulges in tirades against government, but he glumly organizes the revolutionary forces for actual battle. Lastly, Turgenef arrives at the highest type of the warrior, at Sophia Perofskya; and this his last type he paints in brief epilogue, just as his first type he had painted in brief prologue. What this his last type meant to Turgenef is best seen from the short prose-poem itself.

THE THRESHOLD.

I SEE a huge building; in its front wall a narrow door opens wide; behind the door gloomy darkness. At the high threshold stands a girl, a Russian girl.

Frost waves from that impenetrable darkness, and with the icy breeze comes forth from the depth of the building a slow, hollow voice.

"O thou, eager to step across this threshold, knowest thou what awaits thee?"

"I know," answers the girl.

"Cold, hunger, hatred, ridicule, scorn, insolence, prison, illness, death itself!"

"I know it."

"Complete isolation, loneliness."

"I know it. . . . But I am ready. I shall endure all the sorrows, all the blows."

"Not only at the hands of your enemies, but also at the hands of your family and friends."

"Yes, even at the hands of these."

"'T is well. . . . Are you ready for the sacrifice?"

"Yes."

"For nameless sacrifice? Thou shalt perish;

and not one, not one even shall know whose
memory to honor."

"I need no gratitude nor pity; I need no
name."

"And art thou ready even for — crime?"

The girl dropped her head.

"Yes, even for crime am I ready."

The voice renewed not its questionings forthwith.

"Knowest thou," spake the voice for the last
time, "that thou mayest be disenchanted in thy
ideals, that thou yet mayest come to see that
thou wert misguided, and that thy young life
has been wasted in vain?"

"This also I know, and yet I am ready to
enter."

"Enter, then."

The girl stepped over the threshold, and the
heavy curtain dropped behind her. "Fool!"
some one muttered behind her. "Saint!" came
from somewhere in reply.

15. These, then, were the two leading traits
of this man Turgenef. He had the fighting
temperament of the warrior in his heart, and
the doubting temperament of the philosopher
in his head: to the first he owed the choice
of his road; to the second, the manner of
traversing it. His six great works of art are

all tragedies. Rudin dies a needless death on a barricade; Insarof dies before he even reaches the land he is to liberate; Bazarof dies from accidental blood-poisoning and Nezhdanof dies by his own hand. Here again critics are at hand with an explanation which does not explain. Turgenef, the artist, the poet, the creator, does not know, they say, how to dispose of his heroes at the end of his stories, and he therefore kills them off. The truth, however, is that the sceptic, pessimistic Turgenef could not as an artist faithful to his belief do aught else with his heroes than to let them perish. For to him cruel fate, merciless destiny, was not mere figure of speech, but reality of realities. To Turgenef, life was at bottom a tragedy; and whatever the auspices under which he sent forth his heroes, he felt that sooner or later they must become victims of blind fate, brute force, of the relentlessly grinding, crushing mill of the gods.

16. I have thus attempted to give you an interpretation of Turgenef which perhaps explains not only his life but also the peculiar

direction of his works; not only the vices of his intellect, but also the virtues of his art.

17. For the first great virtue of Turgenef's art is his matchless sense of form, as of a builder, a constructor, an architect. As works of architecture, of design, with porch and balcony, and central body, and roof, all in harmonious proportion, his six novels are un-approachable. There is a perfection of form in them which puts to shame the hopelessly groping attempts at beauty of harmonious form of even the greatest of English men of letters. As a work of architecture, for instance, "Virgin Soil" bears the same relation to the "Mill on the Floss" that the Capitol at Washington bears to the Capitol at Albany. The one is a rounded-out thing of beauty, the other an angular monstrosity. Walter Scott in England, and Mr. Howells in America, are the only English writers of fiction who possess that sense of form which makes Turgenef's art consummate; unfortunately, Walter Scott has long since been discarded as a literary model, and Mr. Howells is not yet even accepted.

18. And the second great virtue of Turgenef's art is the skill with which he contrives
to tell the most with the least number of
words, the skill with which he contrives to
produce the greatest effect with the least ex-
penditure of force. There is a compactness
in his stories which I can only describe as
Emersonian. Of his six great novels, only
one has as many as three hundred pages; of
the other five, not one has over two hundred.
Turgenef's art is thus in striking contrast with
that required by the English standard of three
volumes for every novel. For what is to English and American society the greatest of social virtues was to Turgenef the greatest of
artistic vices. As an artist, Turgenef detested
above all cleverness, — that accomplishment
which possesses to perfection the art of smug-
gling in a whole cartload of chaff under the
blinding glare of a single phosphorescent
thoughtlet; that cleverness which like all
phosphorescent glows can only change into
a sickly paleness at the slightest approach of
God's true sunlight, of the soul's true force.
Of this virtue of compactness his works offer

examples on almost every page ; but nowhere
are its flowers strewn in such abundance as in
his " Diary of a Superfluous Man."

19. This work, though only covering some
sixty pages, written as it was at the age of
thirty-two, when Turgenef stood as yet at the
threshold of his artistic career, is in fact, as it
were, an epitome of all Turgenef's forces as
an artist. While in power of impression it
is the peer of Tolstoy's " Ivan Ilyitsh," with
which it has a striking family resemblance, it
surpasses Tolstoy's sketch in the wealth of
delicately shaded gems of workmanship, which
glow throughout the worklet. (1) In the
small provincial town, for instance, the lion
from St. Petersburg, Prince N., captures the
hearts of all. A ball is given in his honor,
and the prince, says Turgenef, " was encircled
by the host, yes, encircled as England is
encircled by the sea." My ball-giving, my
lion-hunting friend, *thou* knowest the singular
felicity of that one word here, — encircled !
(2) The superfluous man's beloved is at last
seduced by the lionized prince, and she becomes the talk of the town. A good-natured

lieutenant, now first introduced by Turgenef, calls on the wretched man to console him, and the unhappy lover writes in his Diary: "I feared lest he should mention Liza. But my good lieutenant was not a gossip, and, moreover, he despised all women, calling them, God knows why, salad." This is all the description Turgenef devotes to this lieutenant; but this making him despise women under the appellation of half-sour, half-sweet conglomerate of egg-and-vegetable salad, describes the lieutenant in two lines more faithfully than pages of scientific, realistic photography. (3) Before the ruin of poor Liza becomes known, and while the prince, her seducer, is still on the height of lionization, he is challenged to a duel by Liza's faithful lover. The superfluous man wounds the prince's cheek; the prince, who deems his rival unworthy of even a shot, retaliates by firing into the air. Superfluous man is of course crushed, annihilated, and he describes his feelings thus: "Evidently this man was bound to crush me; with this magnanimity of his he slammed me in, just as the lid of the

coffin is slammed down over the corpse."
(4) You think, then, that the sufferings of the
despairing lover as he sees his beloved going
to ruin, into the arms of the seducer, are indescribable? But not to Turgenef. Says again
the superfluous man in his Diary: "When
our sorrows reach a phase in which they
force our whole inside to quake and to
squeak like an overloaded cart, then they
cease to be ridiculous." Verily, only those
who have been shaken to the very depths
of their being can understand the marvellous
fidelity of this image, the soul quaking and
squeaking like an overloaded cart, — all the
more faithful because of its very homeli-
ness. Do not wonder, therefore, when the
last, intensest grief, the consciousness of being crushed by his rival, finds in his Diary the
following expression: (5) "And so I suffered," says the superfluous man, "like a dog
whose hind parts had been crushed in by the
cart-wheel as it passed over him." A more
powerful description of agony, methinks, is
not found even in Gogol's laughter through
tears.

20. And the third great virtue of Turgenef's art is his love of Nature; and here I know not where to look for the like of him, unless to another great master of Russian letters, — to Tolstoy. For Gogol is indeed also a painter, but only a landscape-painter, while Turgenef makes you feel even the breeze of a summer eve.

21. So thrilled is his being with the love of Nature, that all her moods find a ready response in his sensitive soul. The joy of the sunshine, the melancholy of the sky shut down by huge cloud, the grandeur of the thunder, the quiver of the lightning, the glow of the dawn, the babble of the brook, and even the waving of the grass-blade, — all these he reproduces with the fidelity of one who *reveres* Nature. Turgenef has thus at least one element of the highest religiousness, — reverence towards the powers of Nature superior to man; a reverence the possession of which he himself would perhaps have been the first to deny, since consciously he was an irreverent agnostic. But his soul was wiser than his logic; and however dead his head might de-

clare the universe to be, his hand painted it
as if alive. This, for instance, is how he describes a storm : —

" Meanwhile, along with the evening was approaching a thunder-storm. Already ever since
noon the air had been close, and from the distance there was coming a low grumbling. But
now the broad cloud that had long been resting
like a layer of lead on the very edge of the horizon began to grow, and to be visible from behind the trees : the stifling atmosphere began
to tremble more visibly, shaken stronger and
stronger by the approaching thunder ; the wind
rose, howled abruptly through the trees, became still, howled again protractedly, and now
it whistled. A sombre darkness ran over the
ground, chasing swiftly away the last glimmer
of the dawn ; the thick clouds breaking to
pieces suddenly began to float, and drove
through the sky ; now, a slight shower began
to sprinkle, the lightning flared up with a red
flame, and the thunder growled angrily and
heavily."

22. Observe here the felicity of the meta-
phor : the cloud rests, the air trembles and
is soon shaken, the darkness *runs* over the
ground, and the thunder growls in anger.

Only the eye which sees at bottom life in Nature's forces could see them in such vivifying images.

23. Lastly, the fourth great virtue of Turgenef's art is his intense power of sympathy.

24. In the universality of his sympathies he is equalled again only by Tolstoy. Like him he can depict the feelings of a dog, of a bird, with a self-attesting fidelity, as if his nature were at one with theirs; and the one child of creation which man has repeatedly been declared unable to paint truthfully, namely, woman, Turgenef has painted with a grace and faithfulness unapproached even by George Eliot or by George Sand. For Turgenef loved woman as no woman could love her, and his faith in her was unbounded. Hence, when in his " On the Eve " he wishes to give expression to his despair over the *men* of Russia, so that he has to seek the ideal of a patriot not in a Russian, but in a Bulgarian, he still rests the hope of the country on its women; and Helen, Turgenef's noblest conception among women, as Insarof is among men, is not like him a foreigner, but a Rus-

sian. And this is how Turgenef paints the
noblest moment in the life of the noblest of
his women.

25. The poor, prospectless foreigner Insarof discovers that he loves the rich, high-
stationed Helen. He does not know that he
is loved in return, and he decides to depart
without taking even leave of her. They meet,
however, unexpectedly.

"'You come from our house, don't you?'
Helen asked.

"'No, . . . not from your house.'

"'No?' repeated Helen, and tried to smile.
'And is it thus you keep your promise? I have
been expecting you all the morning.'

"'Helen Nikolayevna, I promised nothing
yesterday.'

"Helen tried to smile again, and passed her
hand across her face. Both face and hand were
very pale. 'You intended, then, to depart without taking leave of us?'

"'Yes,' he muttered, almost fiercely.   ‚

"'How, after our acquaintance, after our
talks, after all . . . So, if I had not then met
you here accidentally (her voice began to ring,
and she stopped for a moment) . . . you would
have gone off, and would not have even shaken
my hand in parting; gone off without regret?'

" Insarof turned away. 'Helen Nikolayevna, please don't speak thus. I am, as it is, already not cheerful. Believe me, my decision has cost me great effort. If you knew . . .'

"' I don't wish to know why you depart,' Helen interrupted him, frightened. ' This is evidently necessary. We must evidently part. You would not grieve your friends without cause. But do friends part thus? We are of course friends, are not we ?'

"' No,' said Insarof.

"' How ?' muttered Helen, and her cheeks colored slightly.

" ' Why, that is exactly why I go away, because we are not friends. Don't oblige me to say what I do not wish to tell, what I shall not tell.'

" ' Formerly you used to be frank with me,' Helen spoke up with a slight reproach. ' Do you remember ?'

" ' Then I could be frank; then I had nothing to hide. But now —'

" ' But now ?' asked Helen.

" ' But now . . . But now I must go. Good-by !'

"Had Insarof at this moment raised his eyes to Helen, he would have seen that her whole face shone, — shone the more, the more his face grew gloomy and dark ; but his eyes were stubbornly fixed on the floor.

" 'Well, good-by, Dimitry Nikanorovitch,' she began. 'But since we have met, give me now at least your hand.'

" Insarof started to give her his hand. 'No, I cannot even do that,' he said, and again turned away.

" 'You cannot?'

" 'I cannot. Good-by!' And he started to go out.

" 'Just wait a moment,' she said. 'It seems you are afraid of me. Now, I am braver than you,' she added, with a sudden slight tremor along her whole frame. 'I can tell you . . . do you wish me to tell . . . why you found me here? Do you know where I was going?'

" Insarof looked in surprise at Helen.

" 'I was going to your house.'

" 'To my house?'

" Helen covered her face. 'You wished to compel me to say that I love you,' she whispered — 'there, I have said it.'

" 'Helen!' exclaimed Insarof.

" She took his hands, looked at him, and fell upon his breast.

" He embraced her firmly, and remained silent. There was no need of telling her that he loved her. From his one exclamation, from this instantaneous transformation of the whole man, from the manner in which rose and fell that breast to which she clung so trustfully, from the

manner in which the tips of his fingers touched
her hair, Helen could see that she was loved.
He was silent, but she needed no words. 'He
is here, he loves; what more is there needed?'
The calm of blessedness, the quiet of the undis-
turbed haven, of the attained goal, that heavenly
calm which lends a meaning and a beauty to
death itself, filled her whole being with a godly
wave. She wished nothing, because she possessed everything. 'O my brother, my friend,
my darling!' her lips whispered; and she herself
knew not whose heart it was, his or hers, which
was so sweetly beating and melting away in her
breast.

"But he stood motionless, enclosing in his
firm embrace the young life which had just
given itself entire unto him; he felt on his
breast this new, priceless burden; a feeling of
tenderness, a feeling of gratitude inexpressible,
shivered into dust his hard soul, and tears,
hitherto unknown to him, came to his eyes.

"But she wept not; she only kept repeating:
'O my friend! O my brother!'

"'Then you will go with me everywhere,'
he said to her, some fifteen minutes later, as
before enclosing and supporting her in his
embrace.

"'Everywhere, to the end of the earth; where-
ever you are, there shall I be.'

"'And you are sure you do not deceive your-

self ? You know your parents will never consent
to our marriage ? '

" ' I am not deceiving myself; I know it.'

" ' You know I am poor, almost a beggar ? '

" ' I know it.'

" ' That I am not a Russian, that I am fated
to live beyond Russia, that you will have to
break all your ties with your country and your
family ? '

" ' I know it, I know it.'

" ' You know also that I have devoted my life
to a difficult, thankless task ; that I . . . that
we shall have to expose ourselves not only to
dangers, but to deprivation, and to degradation
perhaps ? '

" I know, I know it all . . . but I love you.'

" ' That you will have to give up all your
babits ; that there alone, among strangers, you
will perhaps have to toil ? '

" She put her hands on his lips. ' I love you,
darling.'

" He began to kiss warmly her narrow, rosy
hand. ₰ Helen did not take her hand from his
lips, and with a kind of childish joy, with laughing curiosity, she watched him covering with
kisses now her hand, now her fingers.

" Suddenly she blushed, and hid her face on
his breast.

" He gently raised up her head and looked
firmly into her eyes.

" 'So God be with you,' he said ; ' be thou my wife both before men and before God.' "

26. These, then, were the numerous great virtues of Turgenef; and they have made him the most enjoyable of artists. But his one great vice, the vice of doubt, the vice of hopelessness, has made him, as a nourisher of the spirit, among the least profitable as a writer.

27. For, O my friends, it cannot be stated too often that whatever puts new strength into the spirit is from the great God, the Good; and whatever takes strength from the spirit is from the great Devil, the Evil. And the things that have ever proved the inexhaustible sources of strength to the soul have been not doubt and despair, but faith and hope, — faith that the destinies of men are guided by love even though guided through the agony of sorrow; faith that behind this appearance of discord and blind fate and brute force there is after all to be found the substance of harmony, of wise forethought, of tender love ; hope, that however terrible the present, the future will yet be one of joy,

one of peace. If reason with its logic can
strengthen this faith, this hope, then welcome
reason, blessed be reason ; but if reason with
its logic can only make me doubt the presence of wisdom, the presence of love, then
begone reason, cursed be reason. Verily, by
their fruits ye shall know them !

28. Turgenef therefore was incapable of
creating a Levin, because he had not the faith
which makes the Levins of Tolstoy possible.
He was filled with the pessimistic woe of the
the world, and believed at bottom that man,
born in sorrow, must also live in sorrow. With
the sublimity of a prophet, Turgenef cries :
" From the inmost depths of the virgin forest, from the eternal depth of the waters,
resounds the same cry of Nature to man :
'I have naught to do with thee. I rule, but
thou — look to thy life, O worm ! '" While
personally he indeed contributed what lay in
his power to alleviate the present ills of men,
he could do naught towards alleviating the
future ills of men ; for he could not inspire
men with hope, since he had none himself.
For hope comes from faith, and Turgenef

was devoid of faith. Turgenef, like another great master of fiction, George Eliot, was a veritable child of the immature age, not of science, of knowledge, but of nescience, of ignorance, of agnosticism ; for it is only ignorance that doubts, and it is true science that believes.

29. I cannot therefore ask you to take leave with me of Turgenef without at least urging you to profit by this one fact in his life. Turgenef failed to reach the highest, the height of Tolstoy, because he failed to free himself from that alone which must forever trammel the soul. He failed to free himself from that fundamental distrust of God which is at bottom of all despair. You, too, my friends, have that distrust. O ye in society who dread the consequences of having one kind word to say, or even one glance of re-cognition to cast at a brother because for-sooth he has not been properly introduced to you, are not ye doubting your own God in your breasts, which acts not in fear of your fellow-men, but in trust of them? And, O ye who refuse to help a begging brother for fear

lest he prove an impostor, are not ye likewise at bottom doubting the God within you which acts through pity to a brother, even though he *do* deceive? Turgenef fell short of the highest because he did not cast off the scepticism of his intellect. Are not ye, my friends, likewise in danger of falling short of the highest because you too do not cast off the scepticism of the heart?

a Sceptic

LECTURE V.

TOLSTOY THE ARTIST.

1. I HAVE stated in the first lecture that the soul of man ever strives onward and upward; that its goal is the establishment of the kingdom of heaven, which consists in reverence before God above, and in love towards man here below. I have stated that of this journey of the soul heavenward, literature is the record; that the various phases of literary development are only so many mile-posts on the road; that after the voices of the singer, of the protester, of the warrior, are hushed, there must be heard what must remain forever the loftiest voice in letters, — the voice of the preacher, the prophet, the inspirer. And I have stated that just as Pushkin is the singer, Gogol the protester, and Turgenef the

fighter, so is Tolstoy in Russian literature the preacher, the inspirer.

2. But just because he is the prophet, the uplifter, the proclaimer, Tolstoy is no longer the *merely* Russian writer. Pushkin is the *Russian* singer, Gogol is the *Russian* protester, and Turgenef is the *Russian* fighter; but Tolstoy is not the inspirer of Russia alone, but of all mankind. Tolstoy has the least of the Russian in him, because he has the most of the man in him; he has the least of the son of the Slav in him, because he has the most of the Son of God in him. The voice of Leo Tolstoy is not the voice of the nineteenth century, but of all centuries; the voice of Leo Tolstoy is not the voice of one land, but of all lands; for the voice of Leo Tolstoy, in short, is the voice of God speaking through man.

3. For, O my friends, there *is* a God in heaven, even though the voices of pessimism and agnosticism be raised never so high against him. There is a God who ruleth over the heavens and over the earth; and he is boundless with space, and everlasting with

time ; and he is sublime with the sky, and he twinkleth with the star ; and he smileth with the sun, and he beameth with the moon ; and he floateth with the cloud, and he saileth with the wind ; he flasheth with the lightning, and resoundeth with the thunder ; he heaveth with the sea, and he dasheth with the surf ; he floweth with the river, and he rusheth with the torrent ; he babbleth with the brook, and he sparkleth with the dew-drop ; he reposeth with the landscape, and he laugheth with the meadow ; he waveth with the tree, and he quivereth with the leaf ; he singeth with the bird, and he buzzeth with the bee ; he roareth with the lion, and he pranceth with the steed ; he crawleth with the worm, and he soareth with the eagle ; he darteth with the porpoise, and he diveth with the fish ; he dwelleth with the loving, and he pleadeth with the hating ; he shineth with the merci- ful, and he aspireth with the prayerful.   He is ever nigh unto men, — he, the Prince of Light !

4. And I say unto ye that the Lord God hath not hid himself from the hearts of men ;

he that spake unto Moses and the prophets, and through them, — he is still nigh. He that spake unto Jesus and the Apostles, and through them, — he is still nigh. He that spake to Mohammed and Luther, and through them, — he is still nigh. He recently spake through Carlyle and through Emerson, and their voices are not yet hushed. And he still speaketh, my friends, through Ruskin in England and through Tolstoy in Russia, as he ever shall speak through all earnest souls who love him with all their heart because they know him, who seek him with all their heart because they know him not. Think not therefore the Lord God hath ceased to speak unto men through men; verily, if men but see to it that there be enough inspired, God will see to it that there be enough inspirers.

5. And of these Heaven-sent inspirers, Tolstoy is the latest. But do not believe that in saying that he is Heaven-sent I attempt to explain aught. The highest is ever inexplicable, and it is the bane of modern science that it is ever ready to explain what cannot

be explained. Before the highest we can only stand dumb; and this has been the feeling of the greatest, because of the humblest, of spirits. The Greek painter, therefore, when about to depict the highest grief of a father, gives up in despair, and veils the father's face; and Meyer von Bremen's grandmother, when confronted with the question from the children whence came that sweet babe in her arms, can only reply, "The storks brought it;" and so I can say to you only, Tolstoy is sent unto men from Heaven.

6. I say he is Heaven-sent, because he came to proclaim not what is ephemeral and perishing, but what is permanent and everlasting. He came to proclaim not the latest theory of gravitation, of molecular vibration, of modes of heat and manners of cold, nor of struggle for existence, nor of supply and demand, nay, not even of scientific charity. He came to proclaim that which was as true in the days of Jesus as it is true in the days of Darwin, — that the life of man can have no meaning unless when guided by obedience to God and love to man. Gravitation, struggle for

existence ! The earth has been spinning
round its parent for ages before man's brain-
kin made the marvellous discovery that God's
mysterious impulse which set the earth whirling through the abysses of space is explained
in right scientific fashion by labelling it gravitation. This green earth has rolled on, this
green earth will roll on, label or no label;
and the mystery of God men knew not before gravitation, nor do they know it now
with gravitation. Men have for ages been
multiplying under the blessing of God, and
loving one another, long before that marvellous discovery was made that man, sprung
from a monkey, and bred in struggle for existence, is destined at last, under fine progress
of species, to become brutalized with Malthu-
sian law as a cannibal living on the flesh of
his brother, with self-respect and scientific
charity in most abundant supply and demand.
Tolstoy came to proclaim not the new gospel
of death, but the old gospel of life; not the
new gospel of struggle for existence, but the
old gospel of helpfulness for existence; not
the new gospel of competition, but the old

gospel of brotherhood. Tolstoy came to proclaim the gospel of God, the gospel of man,
the gospel of Christ, the gospel of Socrates,
the gospel of Epictetus, of Aurelius, of Carlyle, of Emerson,—the gospel of reverence
before God and love to man, which is indeed
ever old, but which, alas ! the sons of Darkness
see to it that it remain forever new.

7. These, then, are the men among whom
Tolstoy belongs : which of these the greater,
which of these the less?   My friends, when
we arrive at these, we are no longer among
the measurable planets, but among the immeasurable fixed stars. Sirius flashes indeed
with greater splendor than Vega, and Vega
than Arcturus, and Arcturus than Capella,
and Capella flashes with greater splendor than
Aldebaran ; but who shall undertake to say
which of these suns is the greater, which
is the less? The difference of splendor is
not in the stars themselves, but in our eyes.
And at this our immeasurable distance from
these souls who are nighest unto the throne
of the Most High, it is not for me, the worm,
as I stand before you, to presume to measure

which is the greater, which is the less. Rather than spending our time in profitless weighing and measuring, let me beseech you to bow your heads in awe and gratitude, praising God for the mercy which sendeth now and then unto men the living voice, the helping voice.

8. Tolstoy, therefore, is one of those spirits whom I cannot approach with the dissecting-knife, as the critic does the author, in order to " account " for him. To do this, that total freedom from sentiment is required which was possessed by the enterprising reporter who on the death of a prominent citizen forthwith requested an interview with " corpse's uncle." In an age when sentiment has become a byword of impotence, and the heart has become a mere force-pump for the blood ; in an age when charity has to be put in swaddling-clothes lest it injure a brother by helping him ; when the poor are preached to by their rich visiting friends, not to make a home for themselves when their love for a mate is born in the heart, but only when it is born in the purse, — in such an age that reporter's freedom from sentiment is indeed a most val-

11

uable acquisition ; but I, alas ! as yet possess
it not ! I shall therefore neither judge the
preacher Tolstoy, nor measure him. I shall
only point out to you to-day wherein he dif-
fers, as he must needs differ, from the rest of
that noble band of the chosen messengers of
God to which he belongs.

9. And the first striking difference is that
Tolstoy is a consummate artist, a creator, in
addition to the great preacher. For Marcus
Aurelius is no artist. He is merely a speaker ;
he delivers his message in plain tongue, un-
adorned, often even unpolished. Epictetus,
equally simple, equally direct with Marcus
Aurelius, comes, however, already adorned
with a certain humor which now and then
sparkles through his serious pages. Ruskin
brings with him quite a respectable load of
artistic baggage ; he brings an incisiveness, a
sarcasm, often a piquancy with him, which
makes him entertaining besides inspiring.
Emerson and Carlyle bring with them much
that, as artistic work, might, under more favor-
able auspices, have been worth saving for its
own sake : the one brings a grace, a sportive-

ness, and a brilliancy which fascinates, the other a fervor, an imagination, a grim-humor, a lightning-flashing, which dazzles. But none of these live in letters because of their art. Were they to depend on this alone, they would quickly perish. They live because of the spirit which worketh through them; so that were you to take the Jeremiah out of Carlyle, the John the Baptist out of Ruskin, and the Solomon out of Emerson, you would deprive them of their literary life. Tolstoy, however, even though the preacher be gone from him, still remains a mighty power in letters because of his art. For not only are his works filled with the highest purpose, — they are also created with the highest art. And I cannot show you this difference any better than by quoting two passages, one from Carlyle, the other from Tolstoy, both treating of the soul's well-nigh noblest emotion, — Repentance.

" On the whole, we make too much of faults. Faults? The greatest of faults, I should say, is to be conscious of none. Readers of the Bible, above all, one would think, might know better.

Who is called there 'the man according to God's own heart'? David, the Hebrew king, had fallen into sins enough ; blackest crimes ; there was no want of sins.   And therefore the unbelievers sneer, and ask, ' Is this the man according to God's own heart?'   The sneer, I must say, seems to be but a shallow one.

"What are faults, what are the outward details of a life, if the inner secret of it, the remorse, temptations, true, often-baffled, never-ending struggle of it be forgotten ? ' It is not in man that walketh to direct his steps.'   Of all acts, is not, for a man, *repentance* the most divine?   The deadliest sin, I say, were the same supercilious consciousness of no sin ; that is death ; the heart so conscious is divorced from sincerity, humility, and fact, — is dead; it is ' pure,' as dead dry sand is pure.

" David's life and history, as written for us in those Psalms of his, I consider to be the truest emblem ever given of man's moral progress and warfare here below.   All earnest men will ever discern in it the faithful struggle of an earnest human soul toward what is good and best. Struggle often baffled, sore baffled, down as into entire wreck; yet a struggle never ended; ever with tears, repentance, true unconquerable purpose begun anew.   Poor human nature ! Is not a man's walking, in truth, always that, — 'a succession of falls ' ?   Man can do no other.

In this wild element of Life, he has to struggle onward; now fallen, deep abased; and ever with tears, repentance, with bleeding heart, he has to rise again, struggle again still onward. That his struggle *be* a faithful, unconquerable one; that is the question of questions. We will put up with many sad details, if the soul of it were true. Details by themselves will never teach us what it is."

10. Powerful as this passage is, I cannot help feeling that Tolstoy has treated the same subject more artistically than Carlyle, by embodying his lesson in objective shape, where Carlyle treats it subjectively. And now listen to Tolstoy : —

THE REPENTING SINNER.

THERE lived in the world a man for seventy years, and all his life he lived in sin. And this man fell ill, and still he did not repent. But when death was nigh, at the last hour, he began to weep, and said, " Lord, as thou hast forgiven the thief on the cross, so do thou forgive me ! " He had scarcely spoken, and away flew his soul. And the sinner's soul began to love God, and, trusting his mercy, came to the gates of heaven.

And the sinner began to knock, and to ask admission into the kingdom of heaven.

And from behind the door he heard a voice: "Who is this knocking for admission into the gates of heaven, and what are the deeds this man in his lifetime has done?"

And the voice of the accuser gave answer, and recounted all the sinful deeds of this man; and of good deeds he named none.

And the voice from behind the door answered: "Sinners cannot enter the kingdom of heaven. Get thee hence!"

Said the sinner: "Lord, I hear thy voice, but I see not thy countenance and know not thy name."

And the voice gave in reply: "I am Peter the Apostle."

Said the sinner: "Have mercy upon me, Apostle Peter; remember the weakness of man, and the mercy of God. Was it not you who was a disciple of Christ, and was it not you who heard from his own lips his teaching, and saw the example of his life? And now remember, when he was weary and sad in spirit, and thrice asked thee not to slumber, but to pray, you slept, because your eyes were heavy, and thrice he found you sleeping. The same of me.

"And remember likewise how thou hast promised to him not to renounce him until thy dying day, and yet thou didst renounce him

thrice when they led him away. The same of
me.

"And remember likewise how crowed the
cock, and thou hast gone forth and wept bit-
terly. The same of me. Not for thee 't is to
refuse me entrance."

And the voice from behind the gates of
heaven was hushed.

And after standing some time, again knocked
the sinner, and asked admittance into the kingdom of heaven.

And from behind the doors there was heard
another voice which spake : " Who is this, and
how has he lived on earth ? "

And the voice of the accuser gave answer,
and repeated all the evil deeds of the sinner ;
and of the good deeds he named none.

And the voice from behind the door called :
"Get thee hence. Sinners such as thou cannot
live with us in Paradise."

Said the sinner : " Lord, thy voice I hear,
but thy face I see not, and thy name I know
not."

And the voice said unto him : " I am David,
the king and the prophet." But the sinner
despaired not, nor went he away from the
gates of heaven, but spake as follows : "Have
mercy upon me, King David, and think of the
weakness of man and the mercy of God. God
loved thee and raised thee up before men. Thine

was all, — a kingdom, and glory, and riches, and
wives, and children; yet when thou didst espy
from thy roof the wife of a poor man, sin betook
thee, and thou hast taken the wife of Uriah, and
himself hast thou slain by the sword of the
Ammonites. Thou, a rich man, hast taken his
last lamb from the poor man, and hast slain the
owner himself. The same of me!

"And think further how thou hast repented,
and said: 'I confess my guilt, and repent of my
sin.' The same of me. Not for thee 't is to refuse me entrance."

And the voice behind the door was hushed.

And after standing some time, again knocked
the sinner, and asked admission into the kingdom of heaven. And from behind the doors
was heard a third voice which spake: "Who is
this, and how hath he lived on earth?"

And for the third time the voice of the accuser recounted the evil deeds of the man, but
of the good he named none.

And the voice from behind the door gave in
answer: "Get thee hence! The kingdom of
heaven not by a sinner can be entered."

And replied the sinner: "Thy voice I hear,
but thy face I see not, and thy name I know
not."

Answered the voice: "I am John, the beloved disciple of Christ."

And rejoiced the sinner, and spake: "Now

verily shall I be let in. Peter and David shall admit me because they know the weakness of man, and the grace of God ; but thou shalt admit me because thou hast much love. For hast thou not writ in thy book, O John, that God is Love, and that whosoever knoweth not Love, knoweth not God? Wert not thou he that spake in his old age unto men only this one word: ' Brethren, love ye one another ' ? How then shalt thou now hate me and drive me hence ? Either renounce thine own words, or learn to love me, and admit me into the kingdom of heaven."

And the gates of heaven opened, and John embraced the repenting sinner, and admitted him into the kingdom of heaven.

11. Tolstoy, then, is the sole example among men of the harmonious combination of loftiest aspiration with highest artistic skill. Tolstoy sees in himself only the preacher, and therefore at the age of sixty he does not hesitate to repudiate all those works of his which are not those of the preacher, however great their value as works of art. Turgenef sees in him only the artist, and therefore beseeches from his death-bed his fellow-craftsman to give himself back to the forsaken art. Both

are here right, both are here wrong. For each sees only one side, while Tolstoy is nei- ther the preacher alone nor the artist alone. Tolstoy, like Janus of old, is two-faced, — the artist, when his soul is in a state of war; the preacher, when his soul is in a state of peace. Turgenef looks only upon the face of the artist; Tolstoy looks out into the world with the face of the preacher.

12. This noble combination of the preacher and the artist has accordingly determined the character of Tolstoy's art. For the first ques- tion Tolstoy asks of every event, of every phenomenon he has to depict, is, What effect has this on the soul of man; what bearing has this on the life of man; what, in short, is its moral meaning? Hence when Tolstoy paints, he paints not only objectively, but also subjectively. In the storm-scene, for instance, which I have read you at the first lecture, Tolstoy is not satisfied to give you merely the outward appearance of the storm, its appearance in Nature, he rests not until he has painted also its effect on the soul; and the progress of the terror inspired keeps pace

with the advance of the cloud. Hence the
sudden introduction of the beggar from under
the bridge, with his horrible stump of hand
stretched out as he runs beside the carriage
begging for alms. This incident is as much
part of the storm, and as terrifying to the
little Katenka and the little Lubotshka as the
glare of the lightning and the crash of the
thunder. Tolstoy the artist never sees Nature
with the eyes of the body, but with the eyes
of the spirit; he never sees matter without the
underlying mind; he never sees the object
without its complement, the subject. Tolstoy,
therefore, is the first great artist (and if the
one-eyed prophets of the merely *objective* art
prevail, who now clamor so loudly, he promises, alas! to remain also the last) who has
painted Nature entire. Tolstoy is the first
great artist, therefore, into whose pictures enter not only the details visible, but also the
details invisible. To Tolstoy, the vibration of
the string is not described in completeness
until he has also shown how its music has
made to vibrate not only the air, but also
the soul. Painter then of the inward uni-

verse as well as of the outward, of the
spiritual as well as of the natural, of the
things unseen as well as of those seen, Tolstoy has exhausted Nature. He has plunged
into her nethermost depths, like Schiller's
diver, and lo ! forth he comes from the abyss
with her swallowed-up treasure. Verily, here
Tolstoy is unapproachable. Only one other
man of letters hath here even distant fellowship with him, and this is Ralph Waldo
Emerson.

13. That an art which is born of such a
union of the preacher with the worshipper of
beauty as it exists in Tolstoy, can only be of
the highest, and must be of the highest, I
therefore no longer hesitate to affirm. Read,
therefore, in this light the successive chapters in
Book VII. of " Anna Karenina," where is told
the birth of a son to Kitty and Levin. Our
modern apostles of the gospel of fidelity at all
hazards, even though it be the fidelity of dirt,
would have here made you look at the blood,
at the towels, at the bowls, at the bottles,
would have made you smell the odors,—
they would have recounted to you all those

details which, however pathetic to those
doomed to be by-standers in the sick-room,
can only be nauseating to those out of the
sick-room. Tolstoy the preacher is im-
pressed with the immeasurable pain which at-
tends the entrance into the world of a newly-
born human soul, — agony unendurable, all
the more unendurable because inexplicable,
inscrutable. His great artistic soul rests not
until it hath relieved itself with at least a cry
over such sorrow. Paint it therefore he must;
but he paints it, observe, not directly, by
photographing the tortures of Kitty, but in-
directly, by picturing the agony of Levin; for
the one would have only nauseated, the other
stirs the reader to his very depths. The husband suffers more than the wife, because he
sees her not with the eyes of the head, but
with the eyes of the heart; the groans of
Kitty, which reach him from the neighboring chamber, can indeed be silenced by the
physician's drug; but no drug can silence the
groan of Levin, for it is pressed out by the
agony, not of the body, but by the agony of
the soul. And as love, sympathy, is ever an

eye-opener, so here Tolstoy, the consummate artist, has reproduced the scene of the sick-room with the highest fidelity, because he has reproduced it not with the arts of cold mechanical photography, but with those of warm, sympathetic imagination. Tolstoy reproduces therefore with the highest faithfulness because he too sees not with the eye of the head, but with the eye of the heart.

14. And for the highest example of such art I will venture to read to you the passage in which Tolstoy tells of Anna Karenina's fall. Until the reader comes to this passage, there is not a syllable to tell him that she *has* fallen. Observe then Tolstoy's manner of telling it. I venture to think it far more faithful than any realistic art could have made it by furnishing details not necessarily more true because less delicate : —

" That in which during almost a whole year consisted the one, exclusive longing of Vronsky's life, that which had supplanted all his former wishes, that which to Anna had been a dream of impossible, terrible, yet for this reason all the more fascinating happiness, — this

wish was at last gratified. Pale, with his lower
jaw trembling, he stood over her and begged
her to quiet herself, not knowing himself how
and what.

"'Anna, Anna,' he spake with trembling
voice. 'Anna, for God's sake!'

"But the louder he spake, the lower sank her
head, once proud and glad, now abased; she
now crouched, and was sinking from the sofa,
where she had been sitting, to the floor, at his
feet. She would have fallen on the carpet had
he not supported her. 'O my God, forgive
me!' she sobbed, and pressed his hands to her
breast.

"So criminal and so guilty she felt herself,
that the only thing left her was to humiliate herself and to beg forgiveness. But now she had
no one in life left her but him, and to him she
turns with prayer for forgiveness. As she gazed
at him she physically felt her degradation, and
she could say nothing more. And he on his
part felt what a murderer must feel when beholding the body he has just deprived of its life.
This body, deprived by him of its life, was their
love, the first period of their love. There was
something horrible and repulsive in the memory
of that which was purchased at the terrible price
of shame. The shame of her moral nakedness
was stifling to her, and this stifling feeling communicated itself also to him. But, in spite of

all the horror before the body of the slain, the body must be cut into pieces, must be hidden away, and use must be made of what the murderer had obtained by his murder.

"And as the murderer with fierceness, almost with passion, throws himself upon the body and drags it and hacks it, so he too kept covering with kisses her face and her shoulders. She kept his hand and moved not. Yes, these kisses, — this it was which was bought with this her shame. 'Yes, and this one hand which will always be mine is the hand of my — confederate.' She raised this hand and kissed it. He dropped on his knees and wished to see her face, but she hid her face and said naught. At last, as if making an effort over herself, she rose and pushed him away. Her face was indeed as handsome as ever, but it was now pitiful all the more.

"''T is all ended,' she said. 'I have nothing left but thee. Remember this.'

"'I cannot help remembering what constitutes my life. For one minute of this blessedness . . .'

"'Blessedness!' she uttered with terror and disgust, and her terror communicated itself to him. 'For God's sake, not a word, not one word more!'

"She quickly rose and turned away from him.

"'Not another word,' she repeated; and with

an expression strange to him, with an expression of cold despair on her face, she parted from him. She felt that at this moment she could not express in words her feeling of shame, joy, and terror before this entrance into a new life, and she did not wish to speak of it, to lower that feeling with inexact words. But even later, on the morrow, and on the third day, she not only could find no words for expressing the whole complexity of these feelings, but she could not find even thoughts, in revolving which she might clearly define to herself whatever was going on in her soul.

"She said to herself, 'No, I cannot think this out now; later, when I shall be more calm.' But this calmness for her thoughts never came; whenever the thought came to her of what she had done, and of what was to become of her, and of what she must do, terror came upon her, and she drove away these thoughts.

"'Later, later,' she repeated, 'when I am more calm.'

"But in sleep, when she had no control over her thoughts, her situation appeared to her in all its ugly nakedness. One dream came to her almost nightly. She dreamed that both were her husbands, that both were spending upon her their caresses. Alexei Alexandrovitsh cried as he kissed her hands, and said, 'Ah, how good this is!' And Alexei Vronsky was there, and

he also was her husband. And she wondered
why all this had hitherto seemed to her impossible, and explained to them laughingly how
simple all this was, and that now they were both
content and happy. But the dream oppressed
her like an Alp, and she awoke every time in
terror."

15. And of such unapproachable art the
examples in Tolstoy are well-nigh innumerable. There is hardly a single work of Tolstoy in which he does not display that
marvellous fidelity which has made Mr.
Howells exclaim : "This is not a picture of
life, but life itself !" And this fidelity Tolstoy attains not so much by depicting the
event itself as by depicting its effect on the
soul ; just as the silent sight of the wounded
on the field tells of the battle more loudly
than the thunder of the cannon. I say this is
the highest art, because its method is universal, where all others are only particular ; for
men may indeed differ in the language of the
tongue, but they do not differ in the language of the spirit.

16. Read in the same light, then, his un-

paralleled gallery of life-scenes in "Childhood,
Boyhood, and Youth."   Read in the same
light the death-scene of Count Bezukhoi in(?)
" War and Peace ; " read the war-scene on
the bridge, the wounding of Balkonsky ; read
the skating-scene in " Anna Karenina," the
racing-scene, the meeting between Anna and
her darling Seriozha.   My friends, in the
presence of such art words fail me ; I can
only cry to you, " Read, read, and read ! "
Read humbly, read admiringly.   The reading of Tolstoy in this spirit shall in itself be
unto you an education of your highest artistic
sense.   And when your souls have become
able to be thrilled to their very depths by
the unspeakable beauty of Tolstoy's art, you
will then learn to be ashamed of thought that
for years you sensible folk of Boston have
been capable of allowing, — the Stevensons
with their Hydes, and the Haggards with
their Shes, and even the clumsy Wards with
their ponderous Elsmeres, to steal away under the flag of literature your thoughtful moments.   You will then learn to understand
how it comes to pass that the artistically cold

passionless Mr. Howells even, the apostle of heartlessness in art, — however brave and full of heart the noble man be in actual life, — can be struck with awe before the mighty presence of Tolstoy, and how it is possible ,that the only words he can whisper is, " I cannot say aught ! " The preface of Mr. Howells to Tolstoy's " Sebastopol " has been declared by wiseacres to be the symptom of his decadence. My friends, believe it not. This admiration of Mr. Howells for Tolstoy is verily not the symptom that he is beginning to fall, but rather that he is just beginning to rise.

17. I consider this double-faced presentation, this combination of the subjective method with the objective, as the highest in art, because it is the most comprehensive. Not that Tolstoy is incapable of employing the objective method alone with the highest success ; when he does employ it he is here second to none, not even to Turgenef. Witness for example the following description of the arrival of a railway-train ; still, the essence of Tolstoy's art is the universality with which

he grasps whatever comes under his creative
impulse.

18. Vronsky, engaged in a conversation,
suddenly breaks off. " However," says he,
" here is already the train."

" In truth, in the distance was already whistling the engine. In a few minutes the platform
began to tremble, and puffing with steam driven
downward by the frost, in rolled the engine with
the connecting-rod of its centre wheel slowly
and rhythmically bending in and stretching out,
and with its bowing, well-muffled, frost-covered
engineer. Behind the tender, ever more slowly,
and shaking the platform still more, the express
car came with its baggage and a howling dog.
Lastly, slightly trembling before coming to a
full stop, came up the passenger coaches.

"A smartish, brisk conductor, whistling, before the train came to a full stop jumped off;
and following him began to descend one by one
the impatient passengers, — an officer of the
guard with military bearing and frigid gaze, a
smiling, lively small tradesman with a bag in
his hand, and a peasant with a sack over his
shoulder."

19. And from the same union of the mighty
preacher with the mighty artist springs the
second great characteristic of Tolstoy's art,

that which in contrast to Turgenef's architectural manner I must call Tolstoy's panoramic manner.   I have spoken in the last
lecture of Turgenef as the great architect in
the art of fiction.   Tolstoy is the great panorama painter of fiction.   Of architectural regularity there is little to be found in him, but
not because he lacks the fine sense of proportion of Turgenef, and the sense of beauty
of form, but because his art is of a nature in
which regularity of progress and rigid outline
of form are not required.

20.   Tolstoy's masterpieces therefore are
panoramas, and his art instinctively seeks that
material which easiest lends itself to such
purpose.   Hence his " Cossaks," hence his
" Scenes   before   Sebastopol,"   hence   his
" Nekhludof."   But   a   panorama   needs   no
plot.   Hence his " Childhood, Boyhood, and
Youth " contains not even a trace of a plot.
It is merely a series of pictures, each indeed
in itself a thing of unspeakable beauty, but
all grouped in such a manner as to give col-
lectively a panorama of the entire growth of a
human soul from the moment it ceases to be

animal until it becomes man. In a panorama
it matters little where each particular group is
placed ; just as in Kaulbach's " Era of the
Reformation " it matters little whether the
figure of Luther is on the left or on the right.
" War and Peace " is thus like the Battle of
Gettysburg, a vast panorama, and " Anna
Karenina " is a vast panorama ; the one is
a panorama of the political life of the State,
the other is a panorama of the spiritual life of
the individual.   But a panorama requires not
so much plots as groups; hence "War and
Peace " is not one story, but three stories ;
and each is the story not of one person or
of one pair, but of a group of persons, of a
group of pairs.   And the same necessity we
see in " Anna Karenina ; " here again Tolstoy's materials are not persons but groups.
Viewed as a work of architecture, the book
seems to lack form, the author seems to lack
the sense of proportion ; for the book could
be easily split into two different novels, — the
novel of Levin and Kitty on the one hand,
and the novel of Vronsky and Anna on the
other.   As works of architecture, neither would

suffer if severed from the other. But as a panorama of the unfolding of heaven in the soul of Levin, and of hell in the soul of Anna, the story of Kitty and Levin cannot be read apart from the story of Anna and Vronsky and still remain a unit, and still remain intelligible.

21. This fact of Tolstoy's art being essentially panoramic and not architectural, accounts for the vast expanse of his two great works, "War and Peace" and "Anna Karenina." For it is the very nature of a panorama to be on an extensive scale. The objection therefore made to these two masterpieces that they are too voluminous would indeed be relevant, if they had been conceived as works of architecture; but it is totally irrelevant when applied to a panorama. Which form of art is superior, which inferior, — the concise, compact, rigid severity of the architect's art, or the overflowing, expanding, hence unshackled art of the panorama? Methinks you can best answer this question yourselves by asking another. Which is higher as a work of art, that tender song without

words by Mendelssohn, called " Regret," or
that indescribably affecting capriccio of his
marked as " Opus 33 "?   Which is higher
as a work of art, — that in its sadness unparalleled song of Shakespeare, " Blow, blow,
thou Winter wind," or his " Othello "?   Or
again; which is a higher work of art, a noc-
turne by Chopin, or a sonata by Beethoven;
an Essay by Macaulay, or a " Decline and
Fall " by Gibbon?   Lastly, which is higher as a
work of art, — the wonderfully accurate spirit-
edness of Schreyer's painting of a horse, or
the indescribable power of Wagner's Race
in a Roman Circus?   On its plane each of
the above is indeed of the highest; but that
the one is on a higher plane than the other
few can fail to observe.   For, execution of
design being equal, the broader the scene, the
wider the horizon, the more comprehensive
the view, the higher must be the art.   The
less extended, because more easily compre-
hended, may indeed at first give more pleasure than the second; but if the final arbiter
in art be the amount of immediate pleasure to
be got from it, then Barnum's Circus is indeed

a greater work of art than Emerson's Book, and Mark Twain a greater writer than Carlyle. But if creative power be the final measure of art, execution in the different planes being equal, then Beethoven must rank higher than Chopin, Shakespeare higher than Blanco White, Wagner than Meyer von Bremen, and Tolstoy than Turgenef.

22. " Have you seen any of my later writings? " Tolstoy inquired of a visitor who came to him as the admirer of " The Cossaks," of " War and Peace," of " Anna Karenina." The question referred to his religious writings. .When he was told no, Tolstoy could only exclaim, " Ah, then you do not know me at all. We must then become acquainted." In his " Confession," he is no less emphatic; there he boldly declares the art of which he has been a noble follower for some twenty years,— " balovstvō," foolish waste of time.

23. A most wonderful spectacle is thus presented: on the one hand a writer gaining Shakespearian renown for works he repudiates; on the other, a public reading and admiring him because of the very art he thus

repudiates.   For 't is idle to assert that Tolstoy's religious writings are what draws readers unto him.   Had he published *only* his religious writings, they might have indeed been bought, they might have found their place on parlor table, they might have even occasionally been glanced into ; but read and studied and pondered they would not have been.   For Tolstoy's religious writings, in their spirit, are not one whit different from that of *The* Book which has indeed been for ages lying in the parlors of almost every Christian household ; but it is *not* read, it is *not* discussed, it is *not* talked about, like the latest somersaulting performance of some popular magazine-scribe.   Nay, the surest way to make one's self unavailable nowadays at social gathering of the parlor sort would be to talk therein solemnly of the very book which in so many houses forms such indispensable part of parlor outfit.   Nay, has it not come in society to such a pass that the very presence of *The* Book on parlor table is already an evidence that the host is *not* a member of the circle which looks upon itself as *the* circle, — the select, the exclusive, the highest, in short?

24. The public, then, is interested in Tolstoy the artist more than in the preacher, for the same reason that when Emerson lands in England only a handful of mortals greet him; while when Mr. Sullivan lands in England the streets cannot hold the thousands who flock to receive him. Tolstoy, on the other hand, protests that whosoever looks to him as the artist, sees not him, knows not him ; that he is aught else now ; that mere art, in fact, is to him a business no longer worthy of a serious soul. The public again, in its ever-confident patronizingness, says unto him : " But for thy great artistic genius, O Leo, son of Nicolas, with thy latest religious antics and somersaultings, we would call thee — a crank. But as to a great genius we shall be merciful unto thee, and bear with many a confession, many a cobbled shoe, if thou givest us only more of Olenins, more of Karenins."

25. Who is here right, who is here wrong, — the public with its millions, Tolstoy in his loneliness?

26. That genius should often misunderstand its own strength, and seek it where it is weakest, is indeed no new phenomenon in its history. Frederick the Great prides himself more on his flute-playing than on his kingship; and it is not so very long ago that in our very midst a university professor called the happiest day of his life not that on which he discovered a new Greek particle, but that on which the crew of his university won the boat-race. And a mere chance tour on a Sunday through our churches would quickly show the lamentably frequent misapprehension of genius by itself; for many a fine genius for the actor's art is spoiled by an imaginary call to the pulpit. The presumption therefore is indeed against the great Tolstoy in his dispute with the great public. Still, I venture to side with Tolstoy. I too venture to think that Tolstoy's greatest work is found not so much in his works of pure art as in his works of pure religion; and with God's blessing, my friends, I trust you will see it with me in the next lecture.

LECTURE VI.

———•———

TOLSTOY THE PREACHER.

1. I HAVE stated in the last lecture that Tolstoy is the preacher, not of the new gospel of death, but of the old gospel of life. Tolstoy is to be revered as one of the greatest teachers among men, not so much because he has proved indisputably that only by love alone can men be said truly to live, nor wholly because he shows by logic inexorable that man can be truly blessed only when he devotes his life to the service of his fellow-men. His logic may be bad, his proof may be faulty. To be skilled in the art of fighting with words is no more essential to a noble soul than to be skilled in the art of fighting with fists. Both can indeed knock down an opponent; but knocking down is not the business of life,

but raising up. And Tolstoy is to be revered among teachers because he first of all raises up; because he preaches what those who have raised men up have for ages preached; because he preaches what Christ has preached, what Emerson has preached, what Carlyle has preached, what Ruskin is still preaching, and what will ever continue to be preached as long as there is a God in heaven, and a human soul on earth yearning for the possession of that God. " Socialism, Communism !" men bellow to Tolstoy, and think to confound him with the hateful name. " Would you have us give up," they say, " the fruit of civilization and progress, and return to the primitive life of the days of yore?" But read Emerson's " Miscellanies," Carlyle's " Past and Present," Ruskin's " Fors Clavigera," and see for yourselves whether Tolstoy preaches aught different from these. And if this be communism, if this be socialism, then welcome communism, welcome socialism, because ever welcome brotherhood.

2. Tolstoy is indeed a Russian of the Russians, but he is a man before he is a Russian ;

the greatest of Russians, he is more than a Russian, just as Socrates, the greatest of the Greeks, was more than a Greek ; just as Christ, the greatest of Hebrews, was more than a Hebrew. Socrates was sent not for Greece alone, but for us likewise ; Jesus was sent not for the Jews alone, but for us likewise ; and so Tolstoy is sent not to the Russians alone, but to us likewise.

3. Tolstoy, then, came to deliver a message ; but *the* message of messages has already been delivered well-nigh nineteen hundred years ago. Not one word is there, indeed, to be added to the law laid down in the Sermon on the Mount ; and were men to live out the gospel of Christ, there would be no need of new messengers, the kingdom of heaven would then be veritably established, and the Master would once more dwell with men as he hath foretold. But Christianity, alas ! has been on trial for well-nigh nineteen hundred years, while the religion of Christ still remains to be tried. There is therefore ever need of new apostles to preach the kingdom of heaven, the gospel of Christ ; and it is

Tolstoy's distinction that he came to preach not the new gospel of the nineteenth century, but the old gospel of the first century. For God sees to it that the way to blessedness for men be ever open; that the kingdom of heaven be ever within their reach, if they but choose to enter it, if they but choose not to give themselves over to the Powers of Darkness.

4. I have affirmed in my last lecture, with what articulateness of voice the great God hath seen fit to endow me, that there is a God in heaven who is the Good. And it now, alas! becomes my duty to affirm likewise that beside the great God the Good in heaven, there is also the great Devil the Evil on earth; that beside the great Prince of Light there is also the great Prince of Darkness. And he ruleth neither over the heavens nor over the earth, but he ruleth solely over man. And he graspeth with the greedy, and he splitteth hairs with the lawyers; and he is flirting with scientific charities, and is fortune-hunting with land-grabbers; and he discourseth with politicians, and he puffeth

up with men of science; and he balances himself on ropes with theologians; and he preacheth from pulpits through mouths that have Christ only on their tongues; and he prayeth through lips that know God only through hymns; and he danceth at balls, and he sparkleth through diamonds; and he shineth through gold, and he foameth through wine; and he chatteth insincerely at receptions, and he figureth in society-columns of the public prints; and he shrieketh through steam-whistles, and ·he rusheth sixty miles an hour, and he edits sensational magazines, and he dwelleth with the hating; and he is ever after victims, — he, the Prince of Darkness.

5. And the servants of the Prince of Light are few; and the servants of the Prince of Darkness are many. Yet the Lord God is ever nigh; and he ever sendeth his messengers to call together his wandering, his erring flock. Tolstoy is a messenger sent out to gather together the erring flock back to the fold of Christ.

6. Tolstoy, then, is a teacher of men.

Observe, however, this fundamental difference between Tolstoy and the other great teachers. To Socrates, the great enemy of mankind was ignorance; to him, therefore, to know virtue is to be virtuous, and the central idea of his teaching is— knowledge. The seat of the soul with Socrates, therefore, is not so much in the heart as in the head. To Epictetus, the great enemy of mankind is passion, and the central idea of his teaching is self-control; to Epictetus, then, the seat of the soul is not so much in the head as in the will. To Emerson, the great enemy of mankind is authority, and the central idea of his teaching, therefore, is self-reliance; to Emerson, then, the seat of the soul is not so much in man's will as in man's pride. To Carlyle, the great enemy of mankind is consciousness of self, and the central idea of his teaching is unconsciousness of self, the forgetting, the drowning of self in work. To Carlyle, therefore, the seat of the soul is not so much in man's pride as in his hands. Tolstoy has no such central idea of his own. His central idea is that of his Master, Jesus, which is love. To Jesus, the great enemy of man was hatred, and the seat of the soul to him was neither in the head, nor in the will, nor in the pride, nor in the hands. To Jesus, the seat of the soul was solely in the heart. And Tolstoy proclaims above all the doctrine of Jesus, not because he thinketh lightly of ignorance, not because he thinketh lightly of passion, not because he thinketh lightly of authority, not because he thinketh lightly of self-consciousness, but because he believes that Love conquereth *all* the children of Darkness. Hence the burden of his message is the ever-recurring, Brethren, follow Christ ! Follow Christ with your heads, and your metaphysics will take care of themselves; follow Christ with your will, and your passions will take care of themselves; follow Christ with your hopes, and your self-respect will take care of itself; lastly, follow Christ with your hands, and your work will take care of itself. Tolstoy's book is therefore only the fifth gospel of Christ, and Tolstoy himself is therefore only the thirteenth apostle of Jesus.

7. I must emphasize this fact, my friends, because church-societies are still discussing the propriety of admitting his book into their libraries ; I must emphasize this fact, because hitherto not one preacher of the gospel of Christ has yet ventured to utter one word of greeting, one word of fellowship, to Tolstoy. I must emphasize this fact, because Tolstoy having forsaken art and having betaken himself to the cobbling of shoes, the wise world, that ever knoweth the duty of another better than he doth himself, is forthwith at hand with its estimate, its disapproval, its condemnation. Turgenef therefore gently remonstrates with his fellow-craftsman for his new departure, and beseeches him to return to the forsaken higher field, — to the art of amusing folk already over-amused. The Rev. Mr. Savage, the only servant of God in the pulpits of this great God-fearing city who has even dared to make Tolstoy the subject of a Sunday discourse, respects indeed his character, but boldly declares the man Tolstoy and his Master Jesus of Nazareth to have been teaching impracticable teachings ;

impracticable, indeed, in an age when bank-
stock and a grandfather, and foam and froth,
and social fireworks are the only acceptable
signs of strength.   Mr. Savage, however, follows at least Pope's direction, and damns
with faint praise, while that wee, tiny mani-
kin from that State of Indiana does not even
think this necessary, and therefore, standing
on tiptoe, screeches at the top of his voicelet
to Tolstoy, " Crank, crank ! "

8. But what if in God's eyes there be no
higher work, nor lower work, but merely work ?
What if in God's eyes there be no higher duty,
nor lower duty, but merely duty?   If it be
necessary to chop wood, and sift ashes, and
mend shoes, wherefore should this be a lower
occupation than to thump on the piano, and
read poetry, and write books, and even listen unto lectures?   But the artist is held in
higher esteem than the house-drudge ! What,
then ! shalt thou make the esteem of thy fellows, which is as changeable as the wind, thy
motive for doing, rather than the esteem of
thyself, thy conscience, thy God?   To do all
we ought, be it never so humble, this is doing

the highest work, God's work. But chopping
wood and mending shoes brings no recognition, no esteem, no applause in gorgeously-
lighted parlors, as does the reading and the
singing and the writing for select audiences.
What, shalt thou do thy duty for the sake of
the reward, the mess of pottage it brings, O
wretch?

9. Crank, indeed! My friends, was there
ever a time when the great souls on whom
we must feed, if we are to live at all, were
proclaimed aught else but cranks and nui-
sances? The children of Darkness are ever
abroad, and the messengers of Light are
never welcome unto them. Such a nuisance
was the noblest of the Greeks to his countrymen, that they could not wait for his peaceful departure, even though he was already on
the brink of the grave; and the old man of
seventy had to drink the poison to rid his
fellow-citizens of the burden of his presence.
Of the two noblest sons of Boston, which it
has yet produced in all the two hundred and
fifty years of its existence, one was dragged
through its streets with a rope round his neck,

not by a mob of unkempt anarchists, but by a mob of well-shaven, broadcloth-clad citizens, — by the ancestors, perhaps, of the very men who now can watch the statue of that same Garrison from their plate-glass windows on Commonwealth Avenue. And the other was shunned as an ill-balanced intellect, and abused by those who look upon themselves as *the* best of his townsmen, so that a monument to Wendell Phillips cannot even be thought of at this late day. England's noblest living voice, the voice of John Ruskin, is at this very moment engaged in crying unto his countrymen, "Good my friends, if ye keep on howling at me as ye have done, I shall indeed become insane ; but I assure ye, up to this hour, maugre your vociferous clamoring, I am still in possession of my senses, thank God !" And of America's greatest inspirer, while his gentle spirit was still walking on earth, Jeremiah Mason, the clear-headed man, the far-seeing judge, the practical statesman, could only utter the joke, '*I* don't read Emerson ; my gals do !' And, O ye good people, tell me, I pray ye, what reception

would Christ himself be likely to receive at
the hands of your swallow-tailed butlers, were
he to appear at your doors without silver-
headed cane, without Parisian kid gloves, without engraved pasteboard announcing him to be
the Scion of his Majesty King David? Would
not a mere glance at his bare feet, his flowing
garment, and his untrimmed hair be sufficient
to convince Mr. Butler that for such folk the
lady of the house is never at home, or if at
home, is just about to dress for dinner or to
go out for a drive, and therefore begs to be
excused? Yes, my friends, of the greatest,
of the noblest souls, it has ever been the lot
to be scorned, since their message of light is
ever unwelcome to the children of darkness;
and if against their characters not a word can
be said, recourse must be had to the abuse at
least of their intellects; and Christ and Tolstoy are declared to be weak intellects ! This
is the meaning of the cry raised against Tolstoy as unbalanced, in this latest change of
his life from riches unto poverty.

10. Tolstoy, then, is nothing but a preacher
of Christ; and the first articulate utterance

202 Lectures on Russian Literature.

in his message is therefore that of boundless faith in the practicability of living according to Christ; that of insistence upon the literal following of the words of Christ as a *practical* guide of life.

11. And out of this emphasis of the supremacy of Love comes the second articulate utterance in the message of Tolstoy, which is the supremacy of heart over head as a metaphysical guide of life. For God ever revealeth himself unto men, but he speaketh unto them not through their cold intellects, but through their warm hearts; not through logic, but through love. The reasoner searches God without man and finds him not; the lover finds God within man in his heart, and hath no need of searching him. Hence the following significant utterance of Tolstoy in his " Confession." In his search for the answer to the ever-recurring question, " Wherefore shall I live?" he at last goes abroad to find light: —

" My life abroad, and the intercourse with Europe's most advanced scholars, still more confirmed my faith in perfection as such; for the same faith I now found in them likewise. In me this faith took the same form which it takes in most of the educated men of our time. Its watchword was — progress. Then I thought that this word meant something. Its utter meaninglessness I then could not yet understand. Here I was tormented, like every living soul, with the question, 'How can I better my life?' and I answer, 'Live in accordance with progress.' But this is exactly the answer of a man borne along by wind and tide in a boat. He puts the to him all-important question, 'What direction must I steer for my safety?' and he receives in answer, 'Oh, we are borne along somewhither!'

"All this I did not perceive at the time. Only rarely not my reason but my feeling rebelled against this universal superstition with which men shield themselves against their failure to comprehend the meaning of life. Thus while in Paris the sight of capital punishment revealed to me all the ghastliness of this superstition of progress. When I beheld how the head was severed from the body, and how the one and the other each in turn thumped in the box, I understood not with my reason, but with my whole soul, that no theory of progress, no theory of the reasonableness of our present mode of living, could justify this one deed; that even if all men ever since creation, on whatever theory,

had found that *this* must be, I know that this
need not be; that this is evil; that the judge of
all this, what is good and needful, is not what
men say and do, is not the theory of progress,
but I with my heart."

12. Trust ye, therefore, your heart ere you
trust your logic. Whatever the heart dictates
must be from God, logic or no logic; whatever the heart rebels against must be from
the Devil, reason or no reason. Time never
yet was when the Devil lacked reasons; and
if he can find reasons nowhere else, he at last
finds them in science and in Scripture. Next
to the slaveholders themselves, the last to for-
sake the sinking ship of slavery, were the
preachers of the gospel of the brotherhood
of man, who argued finely from Scripture
twisted for the purpose, that the great God
having made Mr. Preacher white and Mr.
Negro black, had therefore intended that
black shall be the minion of white. Time
never was when reason and logic most inexorable could not find excuse most sufficient for the shedding of blood of brother
by brother, for the burning of village and

town, for the erecting of luxurious palace
within stone's-throw of the homeless.   Time
never was when logic could not show the fine
propriety, nay, the utmost necessity, for competition and struggle for existence; when
men, who might create a paradise of this
green earth of ours, if they but chose to help
one another, transform themselves into pigs,
jostling and pushing one another at the trough,
and grunting with satisfaction abundant at
having driven the weaker piglet off into starvation, — all of which is our modern, *necessary* competition in business; and this is
logical, reasonable, scientific struggle for existence !

13. No, no, my friends, let logic cry never
so loudly at the necessity of struggle for existence, and competition for bread between
men, when the great God hath provided
enough for a hundredfold of the present
number of men if they but chose to help
one another.   The heart saith it is wrong;
and whatever logic makes it out to be right
is accursed, is from the Devil; and it is for ye,
if ye are to become the children of the Prince

of Light, and not the children of the Prince of Darkness, to have none of such logic, and trust the God within you, who dwelleth not in your heads, but in your hearts.

14. And once more, out of this fundamental idea of the supremacy of love and the brotherhood of *all* men, — of all men, observe, — follows the insistence of Tolstoy upon the words of Christ, — " Give to him that asketh." For it is not for man to judge his neighbor, but for God. To Tolstoy, therefore, all men are his brothers, the unworthy as well as the worthy; or rather, he never asks whether they be worthy. To him therefore the law of Christ stands not for utility, nor for fear of consequence, but for mercy and trust in God. Hence Tolstoy would never fear to help from what are branded as sentimental motives. And the third articulate utterance in the message of Tolstoy is therefore the supremacy in charity of the sentiment which comes from God over the logic which comes from the Devil.

15. Relief given from sentimental motives (from mere love of helping for its own

sake) only keeps the pauper population
alive, we are told by our scientific charities.
Heinous, indeed, is the awful crime of keeping pauper population alive ; and heinous, indeed, is the crime of having *any* sentiment of
heart in an age of progress of species and
self-respecting supply and demand. Then
the great God who sendeth his sunshine
and his rain upon members of Associated
Charities as well as upon members of Dis-
sociated Charities, upon the worthy as well
as upon the unworthy, upon the properly
introduced as well as upon the improperly
introduced, — then his beneficence is verily
sentimental. Yes, my friends, the great God
is the great sentimentalist, for he blesseth
men and bestoweth his mercy upon them
not because they are deserving, but because
he loveth to be merciful. When the flower
buddeth forth in the spring with matchless
beauty, no label is tacked on to its stem with
ominous reminder : " Not to be gazed at by
the eyes of the unworthy. All worthy persons, of good moral character, can obtain
tickets by applying to Archangel Michael."

When under His eternal laws the cooling spring babbleth forth merrily from the cave, whispering to the weary, heated wanderer, "Come thou hither, and be refreshed," no sign-board is placed at its entrance: "Beware ! this spring is only for the worthy ; members of the pauper population are warned, under penalty of law, not to trespass on these premises." Verily, I say unto ye, the Lord God is the sentimentalist of sentimentalists !

16. And the Son of God, like unto his Father, was also a sentimentalist. When the sinner came unto him in her distress, he did not inquire for her letters of introduction ; he did not inquire whether she was indorsed in most acceptable society-fashion by the leading ministers of the town. He did not lift the skirts of his garments in scorn of the person unworthy of *his* company; he gave no orders to his butlers that when Madame Sinner calls next he is not at home for her. Nay, Christ did not even send down to the Central Office of the Associated Charities to look up poor sinner's record. Without much parley he stretched forth his holy hand, gave it to

his pauper sister, and with a voice of love spake, " Go thy ways in peace, thou art forgiven !" Verily, I say unto you, Christ was a sentimentalist of sentimentalists.

17. And the father of the prodigal son was only increasing pauperism when he received the unworthy youth with open arms ; he had set a premium (in the words of our scientific charities) upon other sons becoming likewise prodigal.

18. And so is a sentimentalist every noble soul that believeth in God's wisdom more than in man's wisdom ; that believeth more in the power of trust than in the power of fear ; more in mercy than in calculation ; more in charity than in justice ; more in love than in political economy ; more in Christ than in Octavia Hill ; more in the Gospels than in Parliamentary Poor Reports. By their fruits ye shall judge them. If the fear of pauperism result in excusing that vilest of sins, the withholding of help by one brother from another, then away with scientific charity and its talked-of diminution of pauperism ; and if the lending of a helping

14

hand even to the unworthy be the result of sentimentalism, then welcome sentimentalism, blessed be sentimentalism !

19. The obedience to the commands of Christ has thus furnished Tolstoy with a basis for existence which he had hitherto sought in vain from science and metaphysics ; the obedience to the commands of Christ has thus furnished Tolstoy a solution of social problems which he had hitherto sought in vain in ethics and sociology ; and lastly, obedience to the commands of Christ has furnished Tolstoy a solution of financial problems found neither in political economy nor in statistics. And the fourth articulate utterance in the message of Tolstoy is his merciless distinction between the money of the poor, which they have earned by their toil, and the money of the rich, which they have forfeited by their idleness.

20. Tolstoy is thus the preacher, the cause of a change in the hearts of men ; but while he is thus a cause unto others, he himself is likewise an effect of the change which has begun to take place in the hearts of men.   The pos-

sibility of a Tolstoy in the nineteenth century
is the most hopeful sign of the times with re-
gard to the social brotherhood of men. In
theology, the feeling of the equality of men
before God has so permeated the minds of
men, that the claim of superiority which formerly each made over the other, though still
tacitly implied, is now no longer upheld by
sober thinking folk; in politics, too, equality
of men before the law has at last become acknowledged, if not always in practice, at least
in theory. And if monarchies and aristoc-
racies still do exist, it is not because all con-
cerned in the decision have deliberately decided for them, but because it is safer to
endure irrational institutions that are old, than
to undertake the sudden establishment of ra-
tional institutions that are new. Only in the
social field the feeling of the equality of men
has not yet permeated them enough to rouse
their souls against the present division of society into industrial lords on the one hand,
and industrial slaves on the other. That
two men born on the same day, at the same
hour, in the same nakedness, one in a palace

without his merit, the other in a hovel **without** his fault, should each pass his lifetime, **the** one in luxury and idleness, the other in want and toil, is still looked upon by thinking men, by feeling men, as something that must be, as something that should be, since Providence evidently meant men to be thus divided. The idle thus go on enjoying their unearned idleness ; the toiling thus go on enduring their unearned hardship, and all is quiet.

21. Quiet? Alas ! no. Burglars, robbers, tramps, beggars, forgers, defaulters in abundance, jails, prisons, reform-houses, stand out palatially amid lawns and green woods and winding rivers. The silent darkness is occasionally lighted up by the lurid torch of the incendiary, and now and then we are treated to spectacular fireworks with powder and dynamite and bomb.

22. Of course men have *preached* reform ever since God had resolved that however men may refuse to do his will, they shall at least not fail to hear his voice as uttered by his messengers. But though political freedom had been preached by every thinking soul

from Plato to Rousseau, it required an American and a French Revolution to open a path
for the entrance of their ideas into practical life.
Religious freedom, too, had been preached
from the mouth of every soul that had the
genuine love for its kind in its heart. From
Christ to Emerson in our world, to say naught
of the heathen world, the burden of the song
of all saints has been, "Love your neighbor
as ye love yourselves." Your neighbor, observe! Not your Baptist neighbor, nor your
Methodist neighbor, nor even your infidel
neighbor, but your neighbor. Plain as this
teaching is, it still required Inquisitions, Bar-
tholomew nights, and Thirty-Year-Wars, to
establish not even religious brotherhood, but
only religious toleration.

23. Social brotherhood, too, has been
preached for ages, beginning with John the
Baptist, who in answer to the question, What
are we to do? can only say, "Whosoever hath
two coats, let him give one to him that hath
none," and ending with John Ruskin, who,
smarting under the unequal distribution of
wealth, founds his Company of St. George.

Preached then social brotherhood has been, as all else has been preached; but acted out, even under the guise of hypocrisy, it has not yet been. Will this change of heart likewise have to be brought about by blood and slaughter?

24. Tolstoy, in the feeble way of a single man, but in the mighty way of a single soul, giveth unmistakable answer to this question. We must begin the revolution, says he, not without us, with others, but within us, with ourselves; not by force of arms, but by force of love. Of what use are alms handed out with one hand, when with the other we uphold idleness which is the creator of the need of alms? Let each one work, he says, as much as he can, and if he produce more than his own needs, there will ever be enough of the unfortunate and the ailing who cannot produce enough for their own needs. Not leisure, then, idleness, is the haven to be steered for, but work; and work, too, not such as shall pander to the wants of the lazy, but to the wants of the industrious, — work, in short, which shall enable others to

enjoy that labor of the body and that rest of the soul which alone in their union make the perfect life.

25. In his Introduction to " My Religion," Tolstoy says that he has at last tasted that joy and happiness which even death could not take away. He has thus attained true blessedness, that heavenly peace which falls to the lot of all souls from whom love of self and pride of intellect have forever fled. But such heaven can be attained by human soul only through struggle, — struggle often for life and death with sin, with doubt, with faithlessness, with despair. For the fable of Sisyphus is not mere fable ; this ever rolling back of the stone to the hill-top for the tenth, for the hundredth, for the thousandth time, is only the history of the soul on its journey heavenward ; the gold, ere it be freed from the dross, must be scorched, burnt, melted, dissolved ; and the soul, to be made pure in its turn, must be likewise burnt, melted, fused. Think not, therefore, that Shakespeare, ere he wrote " To be or not to be," had been perching on

the tree and warbling right gladly all his days. His sorrow is not indeed found in his plays, but surely it was found in his life. Think not, therefore, that the sportive, merry, joking Socrates was gay through all the seventy years of his life. Not from a gay heart came those words spoken at the end of his days, " We approach truth only in so far as we are removed from life." And lastly, my friends, not from a gay heart flowed that gentle spirit, that boundless love, of the possessor of whom not once, in all the four Gospels, is recorded the fact that he ever laughed! Verily, only through sorrow can be reached the haven of the soul, that union with God which is free from pride of intellect and love of self. And so Tolstoy's life too, ere he attained that heavenly peace, was filled with sorrow immeasurable, sorrow unspeakable. For fifteen years of his life the thought of suicide was not out of his mind for a day; he upon whom Fortune had lavished every gift which in the opinion of the world can alone make man happy, he who had riches, fame, friends, position, admiration, appreciation, — this man Tolstoy has

for years to hide his gun lest he shoot himself,
and his towel lest he hang himself. Wherefore, then, such misery? Because, my friends,
he was natively endowed with a heaven-aspiring soul, between which and the doctrine of
the world there can be no peace. One
must perish, or the other, — either the doctrine of the world, or his soul. His soul,
indeed, was destined not to perish; but the
devil in man dies hard, and for fifty years
the doctrine of the world held in him the
upper hand.

26. Hence though the essence of Tolstoy
is the preacher, he was during these fifty
years never the preacher alone; but this very
struggle in his soul between the powers of
Light on the one hand and the powers of
Darkness on the other is also the reason why
he never remained the artist alone. Like the
thread of Theseus in the labyrinth of Minos,
the preacher's vein is seldom, if ever, absent
from Tolstoy. Hence his "Morning of a
Proprietor," written in 1852, at the age of
twenty-four, is as faithful an account of his
experience as a visitor among the poor as

his " Census of Moscow," written twenty-five years later; hence his " Lutzen," written when he was yet under thirty, is as powerful a plea for the beggar as his " What to Do," written at the end of his career. The final detaching of the preacher from the artist is not therefore a sudden resolve, but the outcome of the life-long struggle of his spirit. The detaching of the preacher from the artist took place therefore in Tolstoy as the detaching of the nourishing kernel takes place from the castaway shell.   When he found his haven and saw that the only meaning of life can be found solely in love of man, and in living and in toiling for him, when the doctrine of the world, in short, was defeated by the soul, then the severance of the preacher from the artist becomes complete, the shell is burst, and in all its native nourishingness there at last lies before us what is eternal of Tolstoy, — the writings, not of the artist Tolstoy, but the writings of the preacher Tolstoy.

27. My hearers, my friends, I have now spoken unto ye for well-nigh six hours.   From

the manner in which you have listened unto me, I judge that ye have been entertained, perhaps even instructed. And yet I should feel that I have spoken unto ye to but little purpose, if my words have merely entertained, merely instructed you; for mere entertainment you can find already in abundance elsewhere, — in the circus, in the play-house, in the concert-room, in the magazine, in the wit of the diner-out, and not unto me is it given to compete with these. And mere instruction likewise you can find already in abundance elsewhere, — in the cyclopædias, in the universities, in the libraries, in the Browning-reader; and neither is it given wholly unto me to compete with these. Not, therefore, to amuse, not even wholly to instruct ye, have I come before ye these successive evenings, and asked you to lend me your ear. But I had hoped that on parting from me, as you will this evening, perhaps for aye, you might perhaps carry away with ye also that earnestness of purpose, the absence of which made so barren the muse of Pushkin; that sympathy for a soul struggling upward, the want of which made so cheerless the life of Gogol; that faith in God, the lack of which made so incomplete the life of Turgenef; and lastly, that faith in the commands of Christ, the living out of which makes so inspiring the life of Tolstoy.

28. Would to God, my friends, ye might carry away with ye all these things besides the entertainment, besides even the instruction you may have found here. In the days of old the great God was ready to save from perdition a whole city of sinners if only ten righteous men could be found within its walls; and so shall I feel amply repaid for my toil, if of the large number who have listened unto me at least ten leave me with the feeling that they have got from my words something more than mere entertainment, something more than mere instruction.

THE END.

G

3

Lightning Source UK Ltd.
Milton Keynes UK
UKHW02f0806191117
312964UK00005B/20/P